BUILDING *in* MINECRAFT

THE *UNOFFICIAL* BUILDING GUIDE TO MINECRAFT & OTHER GAMES

FALL RIVER PRESS

New York

This 2014 edition printed for Barnes & Noble, Inc.

Copyright © 2014 by Triumph Books LLC

No part of this publication may be reproduced, stored in a retrieval system, or transmitted in any form by any means, electronic, mechanical, photocopying, or otherwise, without prior written permission of the publisher, Triumph Books LLC, 814 North Franklin Street; Chicago, Illinois 60610.

Printed in U.S.A.
ISBN: 978-1-4351-5833-7

Contents

Minecraft is not like other video games.

Editor's note: About 98% of these builds are available to download online so you can play yourself. For the most part, you will find them at the spectacular and venerable **PlanetMinecraft.com.** Simply go to that site and type the name of the build in, and you should find most of these (the rest can be found through Google pretty easily).

Most games come out, are played for a while and then are set aside by all except the most hardcore fans, or those looking to dabble a bit in the realm of nostalgia. Any new and exciting things that will happen with most games are due to rare updates or, in some cases, bugs being exploited. There are, of course, changes in strategies, but those tend to simply be slight variations on things people were already doing with the game.

After being out for half a decade, it is now clear that Minecraft is not on the same path as these other games. Where almost all other games would now be relegated to the discount bin, picked up by only a few new players here and there, Minecraft has only become more and more played with each passing month. Instead of fading away, Minecraft has outright exploded as it has aged, being released on almost every major gaming platform and gaining millions of new players with each passing year.

There's obviously something about this little blocky, pixelated, lighthearted game that sets it apart from other games. But what is it exactly that makes Minecraft so unique in the gaming world? What keeps players interested for years after first picking it up? Why is Minecraft different?

Minecraft is different because it is not a just a game, it is a medium. Like painting, singing or dancing, Minecraft is a way for people to express themselves. To put out into the world what is in our heads. It is an imagination facilitator like few that have ever come before, and every single day, in fact every single hour of every single day, there is something new being done in this odd little game. Every day, in some corner of the world, someone is tucked away in a bedroom, using the tools of Minecraft to create something entirely unique, entirely new and entirely brilliant.

This book is about sharing those brilliant, new and unique creations that the players of the world have made inside this insanely and, we believe, appropriately popular game.

Inside this book you will find everything from dazzling medieval castles that soar up to meet the sky, to sprawling underwater bases that are so high-tech they give most sci-fi films a run for their money. You will find mind-blowingly enormous structures, cities that will make even the best computers scream for mercy as they try to render their awesomeness and tidy little homes that'll have you envisioning a master architect at work, placing each and every block with care and precision. There will be boats, temples, towns, floating islands, sublime mountainscapes, incredible inventions, addictive mini-games and not just a few dragons.

You will, to put it simply, find a whole lot of amazing creations in this book. These are the builds of the Minecraft universe in all their glory, but we think that they're not just that. To us, and to many of the fans out their, these builds represent what the human mind is capable of dreaming up. They are quite literally the imagination of the world. And they're really, really cool.

Let's dive in.

Where We Live:
Houses & Homes

The first thing almost every Minecrafter builds is a home. Otherwise, Minecraft can be pretty tough (those Creepers ain't gonna stay away out of politeness), and so there's no more appropriate place to start our tour of the Minecraft universe than the houses and homes that our virtual players live in.

Now, while little Dirt hovels and your basic Cobblestone castles are all well and good, classic even, here we've collected some houses and homes that will have your mind teeming with new possibilities for shelters. From painstakingly crafted feudal huts to modern domiciles that look like they belong on the cover of a real-life architecture magazine, here are some of the best homes of Minecraft.

All-in-One House

By MinecraftPG5: This house is truly unique; in fact we've never seen anything like it before. The brilliant and prolific creators at the MinecraftPG5 group have worked their Redstone magic and created a home that features literally everything you could need all in one room.

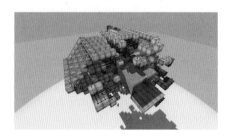

Meant to be buried or to have walls built around its mechanisms (which feature Rails, Pistons and much more), the room looks entirely empty when you walk in. However, push the labeled buttons on the wall and the mechanisms in place will draw back portions of the room to reveal everything from a Bed and a Furnace to a Brewing Stand, Glowstone lighting and more.

Avalon

By SnipperWorm: Part of SnipperWorm's Medieval House Pack, this wonderful little house nails the rustic feel of the feudal era. If it seems like you can only do a great build by going for a massive scale, check out the detail on this rather small build.

The quaint slant of the roof is reminiscent of olden times, when things weren't quite as well built.

The use of raw Wood pieces as actual beams on this house and the nicely done "thatch" style roof complete the image. Best watch out for roving knights and dragons, because this house is quite obviously part of some monarch's ancient kingdom.

Baumhaus

By Porkchop Media: At some point, just about everyone tries a treehouse or so, and it always seems like it will be an easy thing to do. Give it a shot though, and you know that pulling off a house that sits so nicely in a pre-existing tree like the Baumhaus does is rather tricky to pull off.

The key of this build's success lies in the fact that it does not attempt to overbuild. It keeps it simple, preferring a few smaller structures spread across close trees, as opposed to attempting it all in one.

Many builders shy away from using just Wood Planks and building in simple boxes, but the Baumhaus proves that with the right setting, a few extra touches (the well-placed windows) and an eye for overall design, simple can often look spectacular.

Dirt House

By carlotta4th: A Dirt house, you say?! But that's for noobs! We say think again. Dirt houses had a moment not too long back, when experienced builders decided to see what they could do with the material when they tried to make it look good. We think carlotta4th proved that Dirt does not have to a be a, well, dirty word in Minecraft.

Few houses we've seen at all pull off the "outdoors indoors" thing better than this one, and the chickens on the poles outside just give this build an extra kick of awesome.

Franklin's Pad

By boveybrawlers: Some of you may recognize this home from a certain car-stealing related game that came out in 2013. While that house looked awesome in said grand game, we love it even more done up Minecraft style!

The infinity pool, where many a young player has sat and contemplated whether to use his digital sniper rifle on the cars driving by below.

When it comes to accurate builds, this one is pretty scarily perfect. Just look at that wrap-around porch!

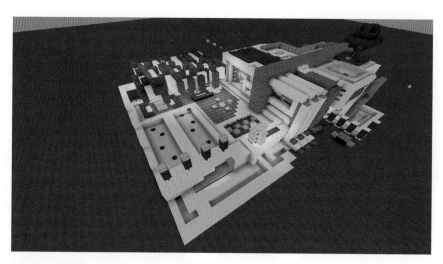

Halo Modern House

By TheHexBox: There are many, many great modern house builders out there, but TheHexBox is one of the true masters of the form. TheHexBox's builds are succinct and creative, often incorporating some very cool natural elements

Not one to leave the inside wanting when the outside is looking great, TheHexBox's interiors are as good as they come. We want this sunken room in our own homes!

One feature that many builders overlook is the value of good lighting placement. TheHexBox, however, does not make that mistake.

Italian Villa

By RaptorAnka: Moving away from the kind-of avant garde or medieval houses we've seen so far is RaptorAnka, who comes strong with this villa done in the Italian style, complete with tiled roof.

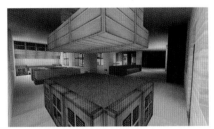

Details are where the devil lies, and this villa is replete with them. This is one of the best-done pool tables we've ever seen, and the hanging lighting makes it complete.

It's easy to mess up outdoor decorations, but RaptorAnka pulls the yard off perfectly with these well-placed artistic blocks and natural elements.

JM Gothic House

By JamziboyMinecraft: In yet another style, JamziboyMinecraft pulls off a house that one could see right at home in an old German town. Using Fences to do the railing at the peak of the house was a great idea, and we'd love to see more of that in other builds.

Many builds, such as this one, are made alone on a flat world. This is because they are meant to be included in your own worlds, which can be done with special methods that can be found online.

Modern Mansion

By skoo: Builder skoo took one of his original attempts at a modern house and re-did it with skills earned over many hours of play into this tidy, gorgeous build complete with pool-spanning front walk and guest house.

The color scheme on this one is particularly great, with the natural green of the (very cool) bordering garden and the outlying Sand playing perfectly against the white, black and gold of the home. The lights under the pool's surface complete the scene perfectly.

Modern Mansion #2

By Pixellicious: Taking a modern mansion and making it larger than just a few rooms quickly gets unwieldy and awkward for most builders, but Pixellicious brought the thunder with this build. A sprawler of a home, it manages to feel realistic and keeps from being confusing through careful planning.

The incorporation of plants into this home brings it to life, as do details like the sunken light fixtures and realistic seating areas. We're guessing Pixellicious has a bit of a history with architecture, though you can get inspiration for your own such builds by looking up images of modern homes online.

NV

By pigonge: Another big boy of a modern build, pigonge has set this mansion apart from the rest by using less white and more colors than many builders use for such homes. The enormous pool (complete with pet Squid) and the underwater portion of this house make it stand out even more.

If that weren't enough, pigonge even went so far as to add a tennis court in!

Seen from above, you can tell that pigonge took the natural landscape into account for this build, something that can take a decent structure and make it truly great.

Shirewood

By PixelBlockMC and NinamanOfficial: This is from what's known as a builder jam in some circles, meaning two builders with different styles got together to make something awesome. These kinds of builds often result in unique structures, like this steampunk-meets-Holland-meets-a-moat home.

Again, notice the addition of natural elements such as trees (which are custom-made) and smoke that really make this build feel alive and working.

Sailor's Hideout

By Shady og Ola: Asymmetry is one of the hardest things to pull off in building, but it's also one of the most attractive when done right. This build seems to us to be right out of the 1800s, and we imagine pirates or other sailors stopping off for a rest here while on a long, long journey.

Here is a good place to talk a bit about a trick for taking screenshots to present your builds to the world: try your builds in various times of day and lighting. You might be surprised when your build looks even better at night...

...or at sunset! Look at that water shimmer.

Serenity

By MrFruitTree: Like TheHexBox, MrFruitTree is one of the world's premier modern house Minecraft builders. Check out the way the decorative beams on the second story window mirror the step-ladder-esque roof of the house.

Plopping down a house in the middle of the ground without blending it somehow into the landscape is okay, but look how much visual work is done by simply bordering this home with some greenery of its own.

Also like TheHexBox, MrFruitTree builds a mean indoor room. Here we see a kitchen, with island, stovetops, ovens and pretty much everything a real-life chef would need!

The Factory

By MrFruitTree: We like MrFruitTree so much, we had to include another house by him. Unlike Serenity, The Factory (perhaps named after Andy Warhol's famous studio?) is a big one, but it manages to somehow still feel tight and efficient.

Part of that efficiency comes from the simple fact that this home was plotted out perfectly, with no wasted space. For instance, this living room avoids the common mistake of feeling too crowded with an ideal pathway that is differentiated from the rest by a change in color.

The repeating white structures interspersed with the brown give this the feel of a compound, where many people could live and work together in a lovely setting.

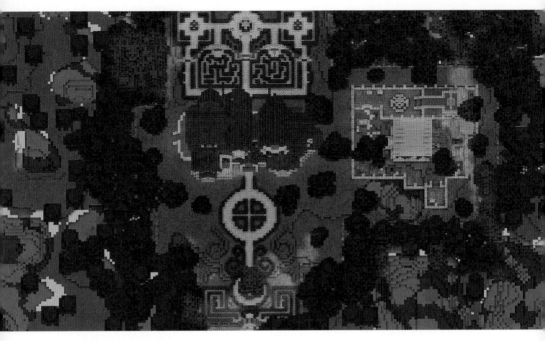

The Hunt

By BjornToBeWild: Actually part of a PvP combat map, we couldn't resist including Bjorn's commanding manor house in our homes section.

This large-acreage build is meant to give players plenty of space to roam around and beat each other senseless in, but instead of just making a standard arena, BjornToBeWild has truly gone the extra mile to make it seem like a realistic country estate.

The gardens in particular are noteworthy for their realism and pleasing aesthetic (though they'd also make great hiding spots for combat!).

Villa Maldiva

By pigonge: Another by pigonge, this villa features their trademark tennis court, but manages to feel very different from their other home by incorporating what feels like human-designed landscaping into the home's property.

This villa has a very eclectic feel without getting too busy. The hanging beams that extend beyond the roof of the house, for instance, break up the monotony of the flat line of the roof without being too noisy.

Now that is a room where a nice party could be had (taking care not to muss up the neat couches, of course!).

The Last Ghost's Bundle

By TheLastGhost06: Part of his bundle pack, this home is actually called Stark 2.0 and is somewhat reminiscent of the famous house from the second Iron Man film. Unlike that modern behemoth, however, this one adds the fun touch of greenery and two pools, one natural and one man-made.

Digital Sprawl:
Cities & Towns

If a home is the first thing a Crafter builds, they tend to start throwing down a few more buildings around that initial one soon after. Get a few of these going, and you've got your very first Minecraft town.

Typically towns built in standard survival mode are a bit wild, being mostly built without a solid plan and out of necessity. Here, however, we're going to show you something different. These are the best of the best when it comes to towns and cities in Minecraft, and they are so well-designed, it's hard to believe their creators didn't hire their local town planner for a little help here and there. Now there's a neat idea!

Al-Hareeq, The Sinking City

By Creative-Node: Creative-Node is a large and very skilled building group that puts out mega builds like this amazing desert city. Like many of the best builds, Al-Hareeq isn't just a plain city-in-a-desert, but is instead infused with a complex mythology that gives it a great personality.

If you're interested, look this one up on PlanetMinecraft.com and give its backstory a good read. It tells a tale of a once-great city that fell into a depression after its mines dried up, leading to its wealth being held by just one man. And then, the dragon came...

Babylon

By Roi_Louis: Taking his cue from ancient history and mythology, Roi_Louis created this quite huge city of Babylon. We love when people are inspired to this degree!

Here you see the famed Hanging Gardens of Babylon done as Roi_Louis imagined they would be, with a Water spouting elephant crowning the absolutely massive structure.

Also included in this amazing build are the real-life Ishtar Gate, the Tower of Babel and the palace of the emperor.

Broville

By Oldshoes and friends: If you want to see what your early-game town could one day turn into, Broville is the perfect example. One of the more widely-distributed maps, Broville starts rather simply, but the farther you go into it, the more complex and cool the builds get.

Broville has gone through many versions, this one being the 10th. Instead of destroying and rebuilding over the same plot, the creators of Broville build in layers, with the oldest sections of town closest to the spawn point.

As a town that was not planned ahead of time, Broville is somewhat confusing and jumbled in places, but that's part of its magic. It would honestly be almost impossible to explore this entire thing, but it is well worth giving it a try.

City Of Troy

By Infinitas_Codex: The Infinitas_Codex group designed this quite realistic looking town, including the sandy mountain behind it that we think completes its image. The City of Troy, like its namesake, has one of the better walls we've ever seen around it. The indentions and crenellations are lovely to the eye, and rather refreshing compared to most plain walls out there.

Desert City

By Jeracraft: This build is right out of the sands of history. It can be pretty easy to fall into a pattern of building the same type of buildings over and over again, but Jeracraft avoids this nicely with the minarets and Islamic-style towers sprouting from this ancient urbanscape.

The sun sets over the desert city...but what awaits when night comes? This map is ideal for creating adventures with friends, especially of the dangerous variety.

Seen from above, you can tell the care the builder(s) went to to make the city look more realistic.

Ferrodwynn Towncenter

By mega_franco: Our favorite question when planning Minecraft builds is "Why not?" That's what we imagine mega_franco and friends said when the suggestion of a town built around an inner circle-moat was brought up, and we're glad they did.

According to the download page, this build has 24 "unique huge and noble houses" plus a secret pirate house somewhere in it.

Take a closer look at the four bridges of the moat, if you get a chance to play this one: each is uniquely designed, but still fits the overall aesthetic.

Forbidden City

By bohtauri: Switching gears a bit, this is the Forbidden City by bohtauri. In what they say is a world-first, this is a 1:1 replica of the actual famed Forbidden City from the Ming and Qing Dynasties that ruled China from Beijing.

The real Forbidden City is 720,000 square meters, and this mind-warping build covers each and every one of them, including all 980 buildings.

Futuristic City

By MCFRArchitect: Another building team, MCFRArchitect set out to create a city that did not look like the other cities that commonly get built in Minecraft, and they succeeded with this thoroughly future-leaning megabuild.

Not one building from this city looks like anything out of our current world, yet somehow the team kept a continuous look throughout each that ties the whole thing together and makes it feel like it could exist.

The whole thing is set up on a series of islands, which include a wide variety of buildings such as a stadium, a university and a partially completed space port.

Greenfield

By THEJESTR and friends: Greenfield calls itself "The most realistic city in Minecraft," and it's hard to argue with that claim when you see it. Incorporating architecture from various periods and laying it out in a semi-grid, Greenfield does feel quite real when you wander its many, many streets.

The crew for this build even went so far as to create realistic roads, including appropriate markings and even touches like underpasses and suspended highways.

It's not all skyscrapers though: Greenfield is a complete town, with residential and other sections as well.

High Rossferry

By Darkone55 and friends: If any city is competing with Greenfield for most realistic, it's got to be High Rossferry. Rossferry is one of those computer-melting builds, in that it is so darn big and full of detail that it can be hard for many computers to even render much of it at a time.

Most of these buildings can actually be gone into, and in the true spirit of Minecraft, the builders have hidden secrets and easter eggs all over town.

In the words of the creators, this build is "what happens when a composer and an architect team up in Minecraft." They go on to say that they are "inspired by great artists. From Van Gogh to Mondriaan. And architects like Mies van der Rohe and Rietveld. There are many references to art, science, music and movies, all over the city."

Imperial City

By Comeon and Rigolo and more: While Rossferry and Greenfield may be competing for most realistic city, Imperial City almost certainly is the most famous Minecraft city out there. If you've seen stunning pictures of a massive old-school city online, it very well may be that you were looking at this city right here.

Imperial City features architectural masterpiece after architectural masterpiece, from immense clock towers to medieval style forts and more, most of which tend to be designed completely from the inside out.

This is one of those builds that can truly be entertaining for hours. As each new chunk renders ahead of you, you'll find yourself growing more and more excited with every step ahead in this wonderful build.

Mattupolis

By mattuFIN and Flowtogo: Almost all of this gigantic city was created by just the two guys mentioned above, which makes it ever more impressive. Mattupolis was built to resemble, but not replicate, modern cities like New York, and it is one of the most gorgeous night-time builds we've seen.

That's not to say it's a slouch during the day either; just look at that sea-green building with the white trim!

Getting creative with street design is something we very much appreciate. Most cities tend to wander aimlessly or be on a straight grid, but using this split road idea is a stroke of genius.

New York City 1940's

By C_B_John: We wouldn't normally include a build that is very unfinished in our best-of book, but though C_B_John has abandoned this project, what he has built is so strong that we had to include it. What this was supposed to end up being was an actual full replica of New York City from the 1940's.

Though only a few sections were completed, the level of detail and accuracy is astounding in this build.

Hopefully someday some enterprising group will pick this one up again and complete it, as we'd love to stroll through a digital Central Park from the comfort of our homes.

Pirate Island

By Heaven_Lord: Minecraftians love pirates (but hey, who doesn't?), but this is maybe our favorite pirate build of all time. Incorporating everything from various ships to coves to one seriously cool pirate town, it's got just about all a swashbuckler could ever need in one build.

There are actually two versions of this map, one of which is just the build, and the other of which incorporates a treasure hunting adventure into the map!

Unfortunately, the adventure version is only available in French, but if you find yourself able to read that lovely language from across the pond, we highly recommend this one for a spot of pirate-y fun.

Sharthur

By RoloFolo and Xtr3m3Shadow: Sharthur is just a downright, plain good medieval city build. One can imagine all sorts of wizardry and intrigue going down in this city, which took just a couple months for its talented builders to put together.

Not quite a castle, not just a tower, we love the way that the two builders played with the idea of fortifications in Sharthur.

The city looks great from above, but you have to explore it for a while to realize that it has a sewer system sprawling beneath it as well!

Steampunk CIty

By Gravi'team: Steampunk and Minecraft go hand-in-hand, and we see quite a few steampunkish city files get passed around, but few have ever been as good as this one.

Set on the side of a cliff, this city has steam pouring out of it at every point. There are even paddle-boats that use steam!

This enormous waterfall is a very good touch. It's actually pretty hard to get one to flow so smoothly, which means these guys really know their stuff.

The City Of Adamantis

By jamdelaney1: When it comes to big, Adamantis features some of the most enormous buildings in the city game. In fact, though these photos show the architecture off nicely, they do not do the scale of this absolutely massive city justice.

What's even crazier to us is that jamdelaney1 built this entire thing alone. Most cities even a fraction this big and complex are built by whole teams, but jamdelaney1 built this in only 3 months.

Various texture packs can really change the look of Adamantis. Here its stark whiteness of the other images is changed up drastically with the use of a colorful texture pack. We thoroughly recommend trying a variety of packs out just to see what difference it makes.

Whaling Town

By JamziboyMinecraft: As much as we love our other builds, it's always nice when someone comes along and skillfully executes a new take on an old idea. With this city, JamziboyMinecraft has ditched the traditional style and gone for a more northern coastal Europe look.

Whaling Town makes us think of mighty Vikings and other such warriors, who spend their lives on the sea and come back to town only for a short while to relax in pubs and see their families.

A platform made out of what we imagine are giant tusks or whale bones. These details are those kind-of spur-of-the-moment ideas that take a build and really elevate it to a status of excellence.

Zarion

By TheVoxelBox (KChamber and Weanut): Part of one of our favorite servers, Zarion is a city in the lands of Thysus on TheVoxelBox. It is somewhat of a steampunk/medieval/pirate mashup that just works, partly due to the gorgeously terraformed landscape about it.

Primary among these landscape features, of course, is the enormous tree in the middle of the city. Large trees are actually pretty darn hard to build right, as it can be difficult to keep track of the overall shape when you're right up on it and building, which makes this even more impressive for its natural shape.

Keeping Out The Creepers:
Castles & Forts

We all know that Creepers are out for us in Minecraft, meaning we need to get ourselves well protected with a few walls and a roof. Houses are all well and good, but when you need protection, you know it's time to put up some serious defense with a solid castle or fort.

Everyone's built ye olde standard castle, with a couple stories, some battlements and a tower or two, but if you want to hide out from that dreaded "sssssss" in style, you'll want to take a look at these most impregnable of fortresses.

Beryl Loch

By QuikFox: A most ancient castle set on a cursed lake, Beryl Loch is meant to be one of the earliest castles ever built. Small compared to some others on our list, Beryl Loch is nonetheless an exemplary project, especially for its weathered look.

The drawbridge and gate both have a very rustic feel to them that is appealing in contrast to the grand, sweeping gates of the typical megacastle (though there's nothing wrong with those either).

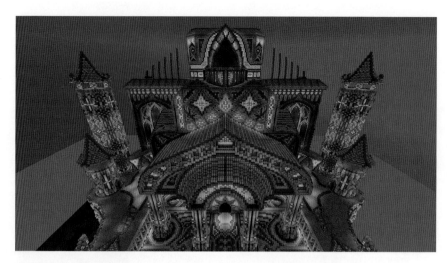

Almor Castle

By playman: According to playman, Almor Castle is around 400 blocks long and 180 tall, making it a whopper of a build. In fact, it's so big that Minecraft could not render the whole thing at once even when the settings were maxed out to 16 chunks.

The architecture and color scheme of Almor are a bit like someone married ancient Catholic building styles with those of a serpentine alien race, which we think is awesome.

Castle Chambord Of The Fallen Kingdoms

By lexa2: Another build whose original purpose was for a PvP game called Fallen Kingdoms, Castle Chambord is more of a classical French castle than your standard medieval fortress. It is multi-layered and very large, coming in around 230,000 blocks.

Castle Hill

By Aandolaf: Aandolaf says that this particular build was inspired by real life castles the Burton Castle and the Neuschwanstein Castle, the last of which was actually the inspiration for the castle from *Sleeping Beauty* in turn.

One thing to take from this build is that it does not leave very many spaces without some form of ornament or decoration, but it also makes sure to retain proper geometric and symmetrical shapes within those decorations.

The particular site for this build was chosen especially for it, but Aandolaf says they had to plant most of the trees and grass by hand.

Castle Svebosin

By RezolutnyDarek: Similar to Aandolaf's Castle Hill, Castle Svebosin is less of a warrior's keep and more of a royal palace designed for the comfort of a lord and/or lady.

The architecture on Svebosin is quite reality-based, taking many of its features straight from real-life structures such as the aforementioned Neuschwanstein Castle.

It seems that RezolutnyDarek is a bit of a student of art history, as they say that Svebosin "is a mixture of few different styles such as gothic, romanesque and renaissance."

Château Le Beef

By thecompound: Whereas our last two castles were more in the style of the 1800s that simply referenced those military castles of past centuries, Château Le Beef is meant to stand impregnable against enemy forces. Or at the least, Creepers.

It's a big one, but thecompound did not shirk their duties when it came to interior decoration, with "almost all rooms decorated."

What can be seen on the surface is only the beginning: Château Le Beef has itself a dungeon!

Dreadfort Palace Pirate Fort

By jefe070: Who says pirates can't have a castle? Not jefe070! The Dreadfort is meant to be the mighty seat of power for a character known as the Pirate Lord of the Iron Shore.

Prettier than most defensible forts, jefe070 made the Dreadfort to look good, but says it contains around 100 cannons including four huge bombardment artillery pieces.

Bottom line: don't mess about with the Dreadfort if you like not having cannons shot at your face.

LEM Castle

By Eventime and LanguageCraft: LEM castle is, frankly, hard to put into perspective without playing it. It outright dwarfs most other castles, with just its outward wall towers as big as the primary tower of most castle builds.

Its pyramidal main keep is striking and enormous, and though you can't see it from these images, the detail on and around the primary buildings is astounding for a build this large.

Were this a real castle, it would hold thousands of rooms and have enough space to be considered a small city itself.

Nordic Fort

By watchmanT: It's always fun when someone builds a standard structure in a different vein than others, and that's what the Nordic Fort is about.

This fort is meant to be a practical, utilitarian style with little in the way of a nod to artifice or decoration, but we still think it looks very nice.

watchmanT was thorough enough in their vision to also do a bit of work on the land around the fort, including shaping a few tall crags to form a valley for the fort.

S'korn Drakas

By Darth_waffle: With so many hillside and waterfront castles, S'korn Drakas comes as a breath of fresh, brimstone-infused air. Darth_waffle says this is a bastion of the dark elves, situated in a precarious position on a fiery lake.

Building in and around lava can be rather tricky, especially when it comes to placing items actually coming out of the lava. Often players use special tools like MCEdit to create such worlds outside of the game and then load them up.

An interesting thing to note here is that S'Korn Drakas loads up in a dark world that does not work great with some special modified visuals, such as shaders and texture packs. Worlds with a specific look like this one need to be tinkered with a bit to get a good screenshot from them.

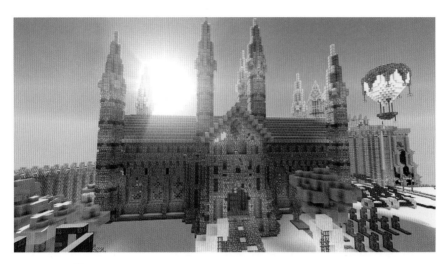

Swordhaven

By Rayman03: When we first loaded up Swordhaven, it started snowing out, and there have been few maps that looked quite as good period as Swordhaven does in a snowstorm. Set in an icy kingdom, Swordhaven is a rather complete castle build, with dozens of rooms, winding passages, courtyards and, yes, a dragon.

The feel of Swordhaven is sort-of Disney-meets-Game-of-Thrones with a little steampunk thrown in for good measure.

As a setting for an adventure, few maps will do you quite as well as Swordhaven, as it manages to be both immediately familiar as a fantasy setting and yet thoroughly set apart from many castle builds by being designed to feel like it's a place that truly could exist.

Temple Of Areatheox

By YanniickZ: We could have put this build in our skybuilds section, but there are so many floating castles out there that it just felt right to include one in our castle-focused section.

Like many of our builds, the Temple goes above and beyond by actually featuring fully completed, gorgeous interiors like this grand rotunda room.

If we had to choose a favorite part of this build, it'd have to be its unique take on tower and wall design. The horn-like protrusions of each of these, plus the rare cross-style roof on the towers are very creative ways to do builds that are almost always done the same monotonous ways.

The Carmine Bodega On The Alabaster Coast

By QuikFox: Some people write little descriptions for their builds, but for the Carmine Bodega, QuikFox wrote the equivalent of a great fantasy short story! This build is all about the mythology, so definitely head over to PlanetMinecraft to give it a peep.

Setting is important in a build, as we always say, and the Bodega nails this concept with its idyllic cliff-side location.

By putting this build on a cliff instead of just on any old patch of ground, QuikFox gave themselves the chance to add flourishes like these areas hanging to the side of the escarpment.

The Eternal Fortress Of Nar

By carloooo: Builder carloooo (one of our favorite builders and Minecraft personalities) is known for his mythical militaristic builds, and the Eternal Fortress is another carloooo build covered in "cannons" and other weaponry to defend itself from attackers.

Despite consistently bringing his A+ exterior game, carloooo is a complete master builder, leaving no interior un-awesomed.

If you'd like to see more of carloooo's work, check out our Hall of Fame at the end of the book!

The Kingdom Of Cipher

By Circleight: Circleight's work is some of the most widely talked about and circulated out there, and for very good reason: she may be the most imaginative builder Minecraft currently has.

Load up one of Circleight's many fantastical realms, and you'll immediately notice that she does not leave any surface plain, choosing instead to absolutely bedeck them in her gorgeous mosaic-style works of art.

And when it comes to scale, few can touch this incredible lady. While we can't suggest more that you download and explore her amazing maps, we warn you: your computer's cooling fan is about to get one heck of a workout.

Thieves' Fort

By mackmo: Also known as Forest Manor, this "castle/mansiony thingy" as mackmo puts it is another example of how it doesn't necessarily take an enormous build to look incredible.

We are especially fond of the clocktower on this build. Most clocktowers get added as an afterthought, usually to builds so big that the effect is greatly diminished, but here it is an integral part of the look of the Thieves' Fort (some pretty successful thieves, these!).

Note once again how the setting adds so much to this scene. Even the addition of a simple road imbues a build with a sense of story and places it in a wider world mentally, tricks that all builders should know and use at will.

Vitruvian Castle

By RezolutnyDarek: This castle is one of the crown jewels of a much larger build by RezolutnyDarek called Vitruvian City. Many builders do this kind of thing, where they release pieces of their bigger builds in order that they get some well-deserved time in the limelight and are available for use in other peoples' worlds without having to take the whole city with it.

According to the builder, this castle is set in the 19th century, specifically being based on Peles Castle in the Carpathian Mountains of Romania.

The styles here, actually more along the lines of the palace types of architecture, are known as Neo-Rennaissance and Gothic Revival, both of which throw back to previous centuries of architecture considered golden ages of the medium.

Vorpal City

By salmon77: Back in feudal times, a castle was rarely seen without a town to support it. Defense from bandits and other attackers was given by the castle to the citizens of its town in return for taxes and labor, and with Vorpal City, we see that style of town done up quite attractively in a steampunk manner.

Warucia Castle

By DJpaulii: It's a bit hard to tell from the photos, but this castle is one of the larger builds in this section. To give Warucia a big of perspective, that decorative bird emblem on the front of the castle is a bit taller than the tallest Oak Tree the game can grow.

Warucia feels unreal in the best way, and as you look at the incredibly high walls and even higher towers of this build, the creators statement that it "cannot be made by humans" seems quite apt.

Perfect symmetry is the star of Warucia, with gorgeous repeating patterns found throughout the entire build. Like Circleight, DJpaulii is not one to let a plain blank wall get into his amazing builds!

Water Temple

By RedJohnxS: It may say temple in the name, but RedJohnxS refers to this build in his description as a "Temple/Fortress complex" he built to be as complex as was possible on a pre-existing island.

This kind of restriction can often lead to some of the best builds, as having something like the borders of an island to work with lets you make creative decisions more quickly than having a totally blank canvas.

RedJohnxS says that he was watching the entire Lord of the Rings trilogy when making these ancient ruins, and the look and feel of the architecture of those films certainly does seem present here.

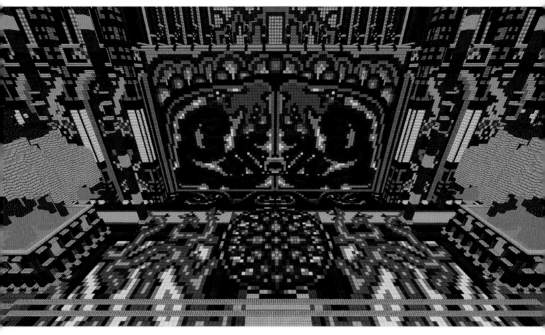

Xehanosia

By Circleight: We just couldn't have this section and be happy with it without another one of Circleight's fantastic builds, this time an absolute riot of a castle called Xehanosia, said "Zay-Uh-No-Sha," according to the download page.

Circleight's builds are infused with not only rich story, but also symbolism and meaning. This particular palace is meant as a tribute to Desino, a destruction god who is a character in one of Circleight's adventure maps.

We keep saying it, but this build is so big that it puts even other behemoths to shame. According to the talented Circleight, it is 1,028 blocks long, 898 wide and a ridiculous 257 tall (ridiculously awesome for a castle, that is).

Underground Wonders:
Caves, Mines & More

It would surprise few players of Minecraft to know that originally the game was known as "Cave Game," as there are just that many darned caves in the thing. In fact, those who play on Survival mode will find themselves spending at least a good half of their time or so wandering the depths of the oft-gorgeous, always dangerous algorithmic cave systems present in our favorite builder.

Thus, it should also surprise few that the creative community has spent countless hours refining said caves and filling their "natural" beauty with a little wonder of their own. Strap on that spee-lunkin' hat friends, because it's time to go cave diving.

Aineuate: Lost City Of Elders

By The Meridian Academy: The Meridian Academy is an exclusive group of builders who each have special skills in various facets of the game, from the creation of textures, to natural forming (terraforming), to even cinematography. Here they brought their skills together in just 2 weeks for a map for PlanetMinecraft's Caved In Contest, and the resulting underground kingdom is downright stunning.

The idea is that this city is part of a lost civilization from "millions of years ago," which was recently uncovered by that hero of Minecraft, Steve himself. It has a bit of an Atlantean feel to it, with the Neptune statue as well as a somewhat Babylonian look to the architecture. On top of that, the terraforming on the caves is top-notch.

Asteria's Abyss

By Hydraxus: Another of our Hall of Fame builders, Hydraxus built this cool, ice-y cave with the help of DJPaulii on the mysidia server, where famous Minecraft people like Circleight can sometimes be found.

The build utilized the excellent Worldedit and Voxelsniper tools, which essentially allow players to sculpt Minecraft worlds in software outside of the game itself.

Such tools, especially Voxelsniper, utilize what are called brushes, which allow players to add and remove blocks in patterns and according to algorithms, instead of doing each individually. This can be exceedingly helpful in creating natural looks like those of the cave walls here.

Heak Colony

By Grery: Caves make pretty good settings for ancient cities, which is what most people build, but Grery decided to take things a slightly different direction with Heak Colony. This particular civilization is set in the year of 4168 and was built by the Svadr people.

As a civilization that wields tremendous technological power, the Svadr were able to build Heak Colony deep underground on a colonized planet, and Grery did a very good job creating a look for the city that feels both high-tech and yet still reminiscent of the traditional soaring Minecraft towers and castles.

This map needs a little bit of help in the lighting area (as per the creator's notes), so it is useful to turn up the brightness on it a bit if you download it.

Icesilia: The Abandoned Mining Village

By The Sentinels Corp: Another Caved In contest entry, this village was supposedly built by a mining group that inexplicably disappeared one day. The Sentinels Corp makes the history of this place feel alive and well by adding in books with the villagers' memories that can be read by the player.

The idea of an abandoned village is strong in the architecture and design as well, which is reminiscent of a partially complete real-life survival mine in Minecraft.

Though not all that enormous, this is a very fun one to explore, especially on the neat little suspended paths and Minecart tracks that criss-cross the caverns.

Serendipity

By persons345: Serendipity is, as the name might suggest, a map that tells a story of perfect timing. The idea is that Steve is but a poor miner, unable to find much but Coal and Gravel in his digging. One day he cracks into this cave and finds these gorgeous abandoned modern homes, as well as an amazing amount of greenery.

Two things about this stand out as quite unique in our estimation: the decision to go modern with the cave build (an unexpected turn, but it works so well!), and the story of Steve turned into a redemption tale. Usually Steve is just a big ole hero, and we like this twist on tradition.

persons345 says that they feel like they might have used too much greenery in this one, but we beg to differ. It has the feel of an underground jungle, and the wildness of the ecosystem pairs nicely with the straight lines and modern feel of the homes.

Svartalfaheimr: City Of The Deep Dwellers

By Thorbanius: Most cave builds feature a few buildings and some plant-life in a large, booming cavern, but such builds are not for Thorbanius. Instead, they took an enormous underground space and carved it out fully in order to put a roofed civilization inside of it.

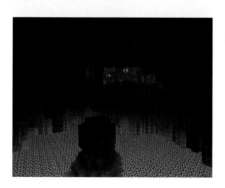

It's a huge build, with halls and galleries and streets spreading in every direction, and the feel of an exotic underground universe is made complete with a seemingly boundless ocean of lava that sits bubbling underneath it all.

The Cavern Of NaKeth

By Turbo_Cass: Lighting is always an issue when it comes to cave builds, as you pretty much have to lay down Glowstone or Torches every few feet to keep the whole thing lit up. Builder Turbo_Cass made this issue moot in their build by coming up with an ingenious hanging lighting system that they use throughout.

In addition to the awesome lighting methods, Turbo_Cass also does some very cool things with the environment here. The walkway bordered river puts images in our heads of the elves who built the city strolling along happily underground, and there are some touches like a giant bundle of tree trunks that are neat little easter eggs to find.

Not just random buildings, the structures in this build are meant to represent actual working storefronts and various necessary parts of a city. That level of commitment to detail is quite admirable.

Underground City

By Twopence: Ditching the idea that a cave town has to be completely buried, with few or no ways out, this Underground City by builder Twopence features a town that decided it would be a bit safer if it used a few natural caves to protect itself from the elements.

This is a fun one because the buildings are much more similar to the traditional medieval town setups of above-ground Minecraft builds than many of our other choices, but these buildings take on a totally new look within these caves.

In addition to the two beautiful natural openings, this city also has an awesome "official" entrance that is fully decked out and gorgeous.

Underground House!

By anttos: To wrap up our underground section of the book, here's a guy who went an entirely different direction with the whole idea. Forget big caves with massive civilizations carved into them, anttos much prefers their cozy, ultra-safe underground house.

The idea behind this home is that the surface is dangerous, full of mobs and griefers that would just love to ruin your quiet home. Why not, then, hide the whole thing underground?

What makes this so great is that anttos included not only everything your Crafter needs to survive (food farms, tree farms, all manner of crafting facilities), but also layers of protection (there's a self-destruct switch!) and some more "human" amenities like a pool. Quite the build!

Aquatic Life:
Underwater Builds

One of the harder things to do in Minecraft, especially in Survival mode, is to build underwater. It's pretty hard to see for one thing, and the physics of the game make it very likely that your build will be flooded with Water at some point, forcing you to do some quick hole plugging.

Of course, anything difficult to do in Minecraft is just an invitation for many players to step in and create something both marvelous and massively impressive just for how difficult it was. Because of that, a good underwater build is a bit of a feather in the cap of a good builder, and here we've gathered together some of the best of those feathers for your viewing pleasure.

Aquabase Atlantian Scale

By MacMasterBlaster: Most of the builds in our book are designed simply to look or do something cool, but this one is slightly different. MacMasterBlaster built this base as a neat starting point for a game that gives you a serious step-up into the world when you first spawn.

It comes complete with all the necessary items to get your world going in a good, solid manner including all needed farms and all the crafting items you could want.

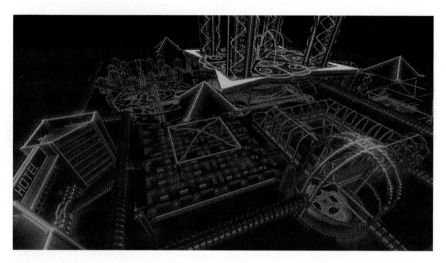

Civitatem Aqua

By janie177: Civitatem Aqua literally means Civilization (of) Water in Latin, and that is no mere brag when it comes to janie177's build. This thing is *incredibly* big, with a massive above-water structure leading to what feels like endless halls and underwater tunnels, each of which is decorated individually.

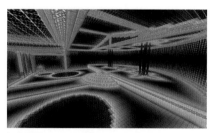

janie177 has an entirely unique take on architecture, choosing to create a sort-of frame out of blocks that is both decorative and functions to hold up the glass, which in turn keeps the Water out of the build.

The goal of this build was quite lofty, with janie177 taking a giant list of the types of rooms they'd like to build and just going at it. Though this is actually the 10th version of the already huge build, there's still a lot left on the list to go!

House In The Water

By Darkscour: This modular build reminds us of something out of Sealab2021 or, for those older Minecraft fans, the film *Leviathan.* Each room serves a different function, and they're all connected to the surface with three different exits.

The tower in the distance is a nice touch, as it gives an excellent viewing area and, if this were real-life, a safe place to keep a look out for attackers from both sea and land.

The mess hall, where sub-surface dwellers could gather to share a meal and watch the fish float by.

Hydros

By LanguageCraft: Hydros was the first underwater map we played for this book, and it remains at the top of our list when it comes to originality and execution of design. Set on and around a tropical island, Hydros is a city that erupts from the surface of the water, with most of it existing deep beneath the waves.

The idea of skyscrapers underwater, some of which break the surface, is a very cool one. Here you see the central hub that serves as one of the primary entrances to the city proper, which goes very deep below what you see.

Ocean Future Of Mankind

By Waterijsje: Many builds are pretty long, but this one puts almost all others to shame at 1000 blocks from end to end. It's meant to be a futuristic/sci-fi style water base, and it looks incredible from the inside, with an interesting mottled floor that seems to perhaps be meant as a sort-of moisture farm or the like.

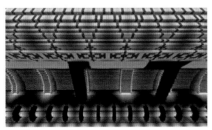

A look at the architecture of the arcing roof, you can see that Waterijsje did not shirk their decoration duties, even going so far as to include a criss-crossing pattern into the roof.

Creating this level of detail underwater is no easy task, and Waterijsje says it took about 3 months to complete the whole shebang.

Satine's Palace

By Antiqua: Now, while this build is absolutely beautifully designed overall, one part of its impressive quality that might not be immediately apparent is that Antiqua had to create not only the amazing palace itself, but also the entire mountain range and lagoon in which the palace proper sits.

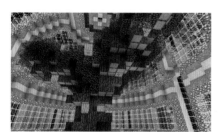

The indoors, crafted mostly by Antiqua's friend Boomer, are gorgeous as well at Satine's palace, with a library and an underwater tree crowning the accomplishment.

It is, however, the entrance to the tunnel that goes from this mountainside, through the rock and all the way down to the seafloor on the other side that is the star of this all-around great build. The concentric pattern is beautiful and not something we've seen much of before. Way to go Antiqua and crew!

Soviet SSGN-941 Typhoon Nuclear Submarine

By Kanovalov: Okay so this one isn't technically entirely underwater, but considering it's a freakin' submarine, we felt like it was a great addition for this section. Based on a quite real Russian sub, this build is not just a pretty outside, but actually features every necessary room inside of it.

The other name for this map is "Tsel' unichtozhena!", which means "Target eliminated" in Russian, but we figured it'd be a bit easier to understand with the title of the sub for all of you non-Russian readers.

Not only does this sub somehow pack everything from crew quarters to missile tubes to engine rooms and more inside its frame (it's one of the most efficient builds we've ever seen), it also features a full crew of Villagers! We're not sure we'd let these guys near a missile if we had a choice though...

Underwater Habitat

By daaw: Blue is the theme of this serene build, which feels somewhat like an underwater casino or a mall with its giant guardian lions.

It's a biggie too, with the focus being on grand ballrooms with views of the surrounding ocean. The basic shader pack for Minecraft will make these windows pretty hard to see through, as Water is not all that clear in Minecraft, but you can change that by using a different shader pack and a modloader like Forge.

Water Village

By kalym: Pirates with an underwater base? We're in! Sort-of a fort/village, this build has a very unique feature in its very large open air entrance guarded by two hulking pirate ships. The entrance just barely breaks the water, so we guess it's a good thing that there aren't any hurricanes in Minecraft (yet!).

A view of the super-neat entrance at night, with guardian ships seen in the background. Something about pirate ships lit up at night just looks awesome, right?

You can see from a far-out distance that there is more to this build than just the awesome entrance; it's a whole underwater compound!

Suspended Animation:
Sky Builds

On the opposite end of the spectrum from our underwater chapter lie those builds that dare to soar, sitting magically above the ground with nothing between but air. One of the neat little nods away from realism that this game makes is to allow players to do just this: build up and then remove blocks from below without the above blocks falling (that is, unless it's Sand or Gravel).

Like pretty much every other thing in this game, this feature has been widely and thoroughly explored and manipulated by players who wish to live among the clouds (read, pretty much everyone). It's become an ongoing informal (and sometimes formal) contest in its own right to see who can create the most interesting and inventive such skybuilds, and that's just what we've collected here.

Aquosia Temple Of The Water God

By mkisner328: So the first time we loaded up Aquosia, we did not know that this map had a bit of a secret...that is until the sun went down. In what we can only assume is made possible by Daylight Sensors and invisible blocks, the huge angel statues in this build will spout Water at night that spirals down and around through the air across the whole temple!

It's pretty beautiful, if we do say so, and it also tells us that mkisner328 must be one darn skilled Minecrafter to both think up such a mechanism *and* make it actually work. The fact that this build floats in the air is just icing on the cake.

Arboreal

By SwitchB0ard: What would you do if you saw a giant, 100+ foot tree floating over you in the air? If you're SwitchB0ard, you'd build a sweet freaking house right up inside it. That's what Arboreal is all about, and though we've seen a few other massive tree builds here and there, that this one floats and also looks pretty great sets it apart in the giant-tree building universe.

This could actually make a very fun survival map, if done correctly. Imagine that you are only able to use what materials are on the islands, and that you had to survive the experience while also achieving a few building goals. You've got plenty of Wood, but that's about it! Why not give it a go?

Elbane's Arrival

By MrD4nny: There are dragons, and then there's Elbane. Taking up the entire 256 blocks that Minecraft can use, this build is a true Bedrock to sky creation, and it is pretty awe-inspiring to stand next to. Even cooler, MrD4nny decided that instead of taking the easy way out and making Elbane hollow, he would actually fill the whole darn thing in, which certainly took a few hours at least.

It's a bit hard to see without the in-game animation, but MrD4nny took the extra step with Elbane to give him glowing eyes. To be honest, we get a bit of a drop in our stomach when this massive guy loads up right next to our tiny player, he's that big and imposing. Think what it would look like with a virtual reality device like the Oculus!

The dragon alone would be worthy of note, but this build does not stop there. No, underneath the dragon, just waiting to see whether it will get stomped flat or be spared by the mighty creature, is the city of Desnig, which is rather well designed in its own right.

Eltrich

By ProjectLOST: A great looking build is not all you get with Eltrich, it's also got a narrative that you can see just by looking at it without even having to read (though you should totally read...we are writers, we do need to keep eating). The story of Eltrich is that this floating town is owned by the rich, who have split their town in half, with the poor living on one side and the rich on the other.

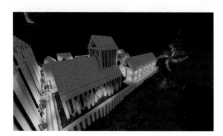

Story aside, the rich side of this town is a real looker, as ProjectLOST has used an almost all-white building scheme that is classical and yet fresh feeling at the same time. Throw in the green of the many plants and it has a very nice color scheme.

Eternal's Haven

By Murps: Okay, we've said it a few times, but there is almost no build we've ever seen that needs to be more looked at in person than Eternal's Haven by the inimitable Murps. For real, this build is *insane,* with something amazing around literally every single corner.

As opposed to some of these other skybuilds, Eternal Haven's entire set of buildings float on their own, for the most part, with the virtual denizens using skybridges and airships to get between.

If you don't already want to download this magnificent map check this out: there is a huge, huge dragon that flies over the whole thing and carries a world on its back complete with buildings! And it has smokestacks coming out of it!

Sky Inn

By CyRRaXxHD: Taking their cue from the Victorian-esque architecture of Bioshock Infinite, CyRRaXxHD created this peaceful little Sky Inn that just sits alone, waiting for weary air travelers to stop by and take a load off.

One of the major features of steampunk is that creators like to show how something does what it does, not just that it does it. This is the case for the Sky Inn as well, which CyRRaXxHD says is powered by "4 Quantum Mechanics powered reactors."

Skytastic!

By reVolusion_minecrXft: Ever since Notch first showed off the then upcoming Minecart addition to the game years ago on his Youtube channel, where he uploaded a video of the first Minecraft roller coaster, people have been doing theme park builds. This theme-park, however, floats in the sky, making it infinitely better than most other contenders. Welcome to Skytastic!

A colorful, fun-themed build, Skytastic! features multiple areas like you might find in a real theme park, including a kid's zone and, of course, a roller coaster or two.

It's not the biggest or flashiest skybuild ever, but we guarantee you'll have a good darn time kicking it at Skytastic!, especially if you bring a friend or two along.

Steve's Evil Tower Of Ominousness

By Ragnur Le Barbare: The skies are often thought of as lighthearted, relaxing places, and the builds in Minecraft tend to go that route in the sky. As the name might give you a clue toward, Steve's Evil Tower of Ominousness is not that kind of build.

There's nothing frilly or fluffy about Ragnur Le Barbare's tower, nor is it all that flashy in terms of color, but it is just one solid tower, with a look all its own and a size that can't be denied. The Lava flows just make it all that much better. This is a build that would look great in another world, perhaps floating its horror above a peasant village below.

Stortic's Skyhouse

By TheCraftMiner: This is one of those kind of builds where we looked at it and said, "Oh! We never thought of doing it that way." We've certainly built a tower or forty in our time, but we never really thought to do it so organically, in a circle with a variety of layers and a plethora of plants about.

It's these kind of quietly creative builds that just take something familiar and turn it into a new design that keep us pushing the limits of our own builds, and it does not hurt that it's absolutely cool looking in any light as well.

Adding the little sub-islands and floating balloons is, as we continue to say, a perfect touch that takes this from just a cool build to a real setting, where a story could take place and might just (with the right players).

Terados Skyland

By Lemon-Fox: Lemon-Fox tells a familiar tale about this build: after spending many many hours on it, the files were corrupted and only the castle remained of what was once a much larger build. The work was set aside for a while out of frustration, but it has a happy ending, as Lemon-Fox and crew returned to it a long while later with newfound skills at crafting, and the results are what you see before you.

From this attractive and well-organized floating city of Terados, we can learn a few lessons: first, always, always, always, always (that's right, four alwayses) make copies of your save files if you do big time builds, or even if not.

And second, keep your old projects around, even if you don't like them anymore or they don't seem great. You never know when you might feel like coming back to them. Builds like these usually end up great, and it's like working with a past version of yourself!

The Charity

By ImACow: Take a sweet fantasy castle, add some sci-fi architecture and some big darn engines and throw it up in the sky, and you've got The Charity. ImACow tells the story of the build thus: they started with a simple Arabic influence, and decided it needed something crazier to spice it up.

So, they added these super-cool sci-fi elements, like these insane and very original engines. Still not content, however, they then went in and did-up all of the insides, including throwing a whole heap of awesome Redstone mechanisms into the mix (give them a try if you download the map!).

Eventually they just went all out, and made every single surface and area as detailed and precisely designed as they could, even going so far as to argue about what kind of trees should be used in each spot! It's a tale of achievement that proves it only takes a simple idea to start, and if you just keep working and caring, you can turn that small idea into something completely new and beautiful.

The Winged Skies

By Kaik_7: This build is just about perfect, in that every single part of it works to support the look and feel of the rest, resulting in a totality that is both beautiful and exciting. Just look at that serpent curling itself around the top of the tower! They did not have to do that, but oh are we glad they did.

Each little island and floating feature around the main structure has its own look and feel, but this is our favorite. Hot air balloons and steampunk airships are common, but we don't think we've ever seen another ship that was a basket strapped to a dragon. We want to ride this thing. Get on it, science.

Zarkhaden's Fortress By skrill94

By skrill94: This isn't exactly a totally-in-the-sky build, but we included it because its floating elements involve some of the cooler patterns we've seen in any build. Most especially, the huge floating mosaic above the primary tower in Zarkhaden's Fortress is a mind-bender.

These little floating towers are no slouches ether! Get up close and see how the symmetrical pattern is created, and you should be able to reproduce it pretty easily in your own builds.

Use Creative mode and get yourself on top of this bad boy when you get a chance. It looks amazing from below, but when you're right up on this awesome mosaic, you can really get a sense of the complexity of the pattern. Outstanding work, folks!

Pixel Geology:
Landscapes & Natural Builds

Now here's something many Crafters don't think about until they see it: structures and items aren't the only things you can make look amazing in Minecraft! You can also turn your focus to the earth itself, using your own imagination and inspiration from beautiful real-life places (or fantastical ones) to craft the very ground and environment.

The builders who focus on this are a very special kind of builder, and not everyone has the patience or the vision to do it right, but when they do create these amazing landscapes, they allow other builders to use these amazing builds in their own worlds. It's a niche, certainly, but an important one, and one that's just as impressive if not sometimes more than more standard styles of play.

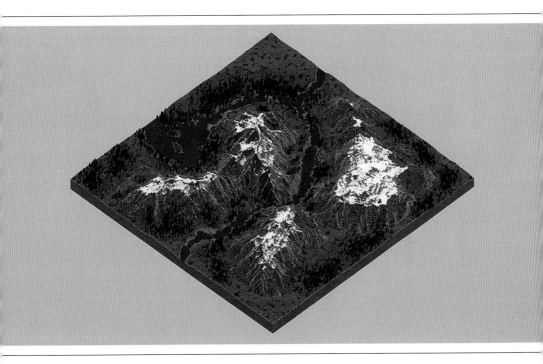

Alpine Valley

By Merlin_Warlock: The Alpine Valley is the definition of sublime: truly massive snowcapped mountains that are split by a deep river valley, complete with appropriate trees and even a little river lake.

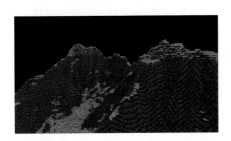

It's the perfect setting for your wizard tower or isolated redoubt, so if you've always wished the mountains were more realistic in Minecraft, this is your map.

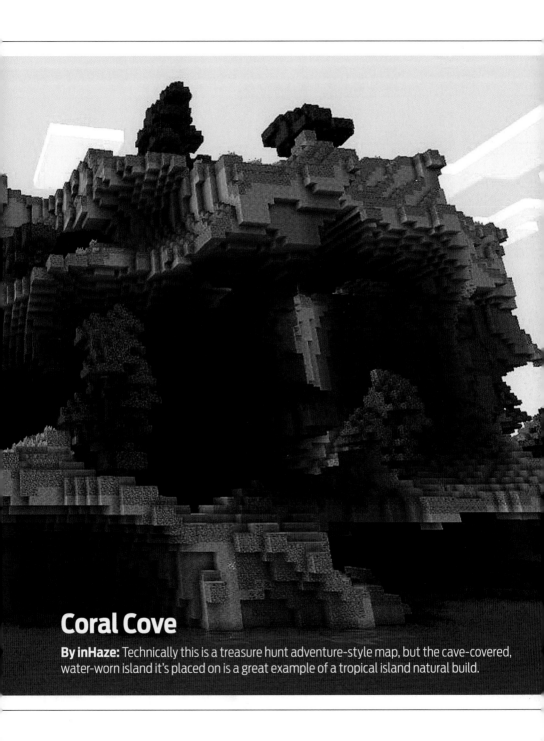

Coral Cove

By inHaze: Technically this is a treasure hunt adventure-style map, but the cave-covered, water-worn island it's placed on is a great example of a tropical island natural build.

Lands of Iuvem

By Corpeh: If one biome style isn't enough for you, you want the Lands of Iuvem in your world. Featuring not just one, not just two, but six separate biomes to build and play in.

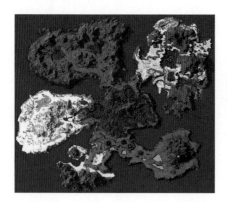

It's hard to tell from these shots, but this map is actually pretty large. In fact, it clocks in at 4000x4000 blocks, meaning there is a surface area of 16 million blocks. That's a lot of room to build!

Realistic Jungle Island

By o00gareth00o: If you saw Coral Cove and thought it wasn't quite wild enough of a land for you, this Realistic Jungle Island sets out to truly capture the look and feel of earth's many jungle islands. It has coves, a couple central spires and a bunch of little reality-based hills as well.

It's really not hard to imagine a pirate town or a beach resort tucked into this island, or you could go all *Tropico* on it and create an entire island nation!

All that greenery is just waiting for a human touch, though it certainly does look nice all pristine and un-chopped-down.

Shattered Land

By inHaze: Another by the great inHaze, this build is quite a bit less realistic than the other natural builds because the lands it features simply couldn't exist in our world's physics. That being said, it's also an excellent example of how natural builds can be massively creative and fantastical while still retaining their focus on the environment.

The Tree Of Kajin

By Techno: Another example of a more fantastical natural approach, Techno's Tree of Kajin is one of the nicest giant trees we've ever seen, especially with those cool hanging vines.

Creator Techno gives a great suggestion in his notes for this map: why not download it and light the thing on fire? Wood and leaves burn in Minecraft, and you're unlikely to see a bigger blaze otherwise in the game.

Vhalar

By GGJ16: If the varied biomes of the Lands of Iuvem were a little too unrealistic, or the map was too small for you, the continent of Vhalar by GGJ16 might be up your alley. This one features life-like biomes in that the snow is in the north, the temperate zones in the middle and the desert in the south.

Even with being as big as it is (7000x5000 blocks), builder GGJ16 has taken the time to really personalize and customize the landscape with fun little details like this one-tree island.

And this gorgeous cove that features multiple bespoke biomes side-by-side.

Building Out Of The Box:
Creative Builds

There are some fairly-to-very common types of builds in Minecraft: cities, houses, castles and cave builds are all rather plentiful. However, these tropes of Minecraft are certainly not the only things that can be done. The rule of Minecraft is that if you can think it up, you can probably make it happen.

That's just what this section is all about- taking ideas that are outside of the standard Minecraft box (Get it? 'Cause they're blocks...yeah never mind, we'll stop.) and showing you what can be done when the basic plans are thrown right out. We'll give you a hint: it's awesomeness. Awesomeness is what happens.

Atropos

By carloooo: The eminent carloooo makes another appearance in our book, this time for a build that when it came out, it had people saying it might just be the best that's ever been done in the game. That's a big claim, but this steampunk battle fortress/turtle/city really is that good.

From its original concept to its painstakingly crafted exterior to the fully decked out and almost more impressive interior, Antropos is a true monument to what Minecraft can be, and it is one of the most creative builds yet done in the history of a game that is all about creation and imagination. carloooo, you are a mighty, might personage, and we agree with you that potatoes are indeed delicious.

Basketball

By AssassinatorRFC: Most people that just have one map up on PlanetMinecraft tend to have something pretty simple and standard, but that's not how AssassinatorRFC rolls. In their lone map on the site, they created one of the best working mini-games ever executed with this awesome, working, competitive Minecraft Basketball Arena. You can actually jump, shoot balls, keep track of your score and even (insanely) block shots! You will have fun with this one, we promise.

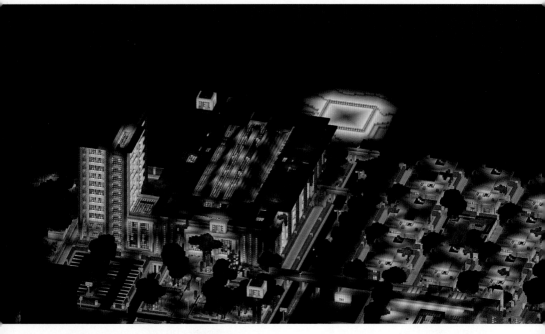

Beach Town Mall

By Kielbasa: Originally located on the famed World of Keralis server, this build is now available for anyone to meander through and maybe do some shopping. While not the biggest or flashiest build, what makes this beach mall so great to us is that it is just so darn close to what real malls look like.

Even the general floor-plan of this build reminds us of our local malls, which means these guys really did their research on the build.

Just tell us you can't image various Crafters strolling about this building picking up some Cake and Anvils. We'd really like to see this one used on a server with actual shops. Quick, young builder! Get on it!

Brinkmoor

By QuikFox: QuikFox is certainly creative, and in fact this little town of Brinkmoor is so original and different that we felt it belonged in this section even over the actual cities chapter. The idea of placing a city not just on a hill or mountain or field, but on the actual side of a cliff is inspired and fun, and it gives us some great ideas for future towns.

QuikFox could have stopped at just the outside of these buildings themselves, as their creativity and setting make them already great, but they went so far as to make it a treat to stroll through this most unique of towns as well.

Conxunto de Vento: The Hanging City

By Huggers: Speaking of creative cities, how about Huggers' Conxunto de Vento, the Hanging City? Having a central spire that is itself very nicely wrought plus taking the awesome mental leap to have the houses and buildings hang down in chains is something we can't get enough of.

It's not perhaps the most practical city for getting about, but what's certain is that no wandering bandits or bears or bees (you know, the three most dangerous things there are) will be getting at any of these citizens' treasures.

This could be a really neat addition to a great natural biome. Imagine these chains of buildings hanging from the top of a mountain, or even inside a cave. Or in space! Yay space!

Costa Concordia

By CharlesGoldburn: CharlesGoldburn is a builder that crafts to beat of his own drum, and that drum is telling him to build boats. As one of the most skilled boat-builders in the game, CharlesGoldburn likes to create 1:1 replicas of famous or real-life boats or boat styles, and that's what he's done with the once-floating Costa Concordia.

You might remember the Costa Concordia as a somewhat famous shipwreck which is actually still located where it wrecked by the island of Gilgio, Italy. In that deadly wreck, a captain ran the ship into a rock, sinking it and causing passenger deaths. This build is, we believe, CharlesGoldburn's monument to those dead, and we think it is a wonderfully accurate build.

CharlesGoldburn is obviously a bit of a boat man in real life, as he has included the following interesting and very nautical facts about his version of the Costa Concordia:

Ship Statistics:
- Length: 290 Blocks
- Width: 37 Blocks
- Draught: 9 Blocks

Cube World V2

By Tyken132: When we saw the Cube World V2, we couldn't believe we'd never thought of recreating the natural world of Minecraft gone sideways. What's required in this build is pretty interesting: Tyken132 had to learn exactly how each natural feature is built by the game's algorithm, and then literally turn those ideas on their side.

The result is nothing less than one of the most fun builds we've ever had the pleasure of seeing. It even includes sideways Lava...

...and Water! Which are nicely held in by glass and look exactly like naturally occurring such pools.

Iration The Submarine City

By loki0841: This would have made it into our underwater section, but since the build itself is (for convenience, we guess) set up above the water, we decided it worked best here. We like to imagine that Iration is a combination air/water city ship, able to move between the two with ease as its citizens desire.

What Iration looks like submerged. Thanks loki0841 for giving us yet another unrealistic dream for an awesome future home.

Despite how amazing the outside of this build is, the indoors are even better. It has a kind-of utopic 70's sci-fi feel to it, with lots of space for citizens to live in. A note- the spiffy shadows on the wall here were created due to shaders, which, once again, we can't recommend enough.

Minecraft Game Show

By Nboss233: You probably recognize this right away, and yes, it's a working version of that in Minecraft. And it is so much fun. Whether alone or, much better, with friends, you owe it to yourself as a player to download this one and see what kind of run you can make.

Unfortunately, *Harry Potter*-esque moving paper images aren't a thing yet, so you can't tell that this whole thing is moving up and down in various patterns with pistons. Yes, to answer your question, it is very hard to get across.

A real triumph of Redstone, concept, mini-games and aesthetic, this Minecraft Game Show map is endless fun and unbelievably hard to get across without falling hilariously at least five or five billion times. It's not in these shots, but there is actually a working giant digital timer that will keep track of your time on your run, plus a little sign to write down the top scores!

Olann Island

By Enmah: This map is possibly one of the top 5 most seen and beloved Minecraft maps ever, in our estimation. There are thousands upon thousands of roller coaster/theme park maps out there, but perhaps because it just looks so good and complete, Olann Island is the top dog.

And it has just about everything you could want in terms of entertainment, including planes, boats, coasters and, as you see here, maybe the nicest looking casino we've come across.

It's a classic for a reason, and we think you'll love hanging out on this little island if you give 'er the ole download from PlanetMinecraft.com.

Vanaheim The City Ship

By Ragnur Le Barbare: If Iration is the sleek, stylized ship to take a small town around the earth as they please, Vanaheim is Iration's big brother in the stars. It's meant to transmit thousands and thousands of people/Miners between the stars, giving them everything they need to not only survive as long a journey as needed, but also to colonize a lucky planet they might happen across.

We like the engines especially on this behemoth, which is so big that we literally could not fit both the engines and even the middle parts of the ship rendered at the same time.

Spaghetti Roller Coaster

By DeliciousPancake: Things you can expect in this western-themed roller coaster map by the builder with our favorite name ever: explosions, 4 minutes on the ride, jugglin', lamps that fly about and a whole, whole lot of sweet steampunk houses. Roller coasters are a genre in and of themselves in Minecraft, and though we didn't have enough space to include a whole section for them (maybe next edition!), we knew this one had to go in the book when we gave it a whirl.

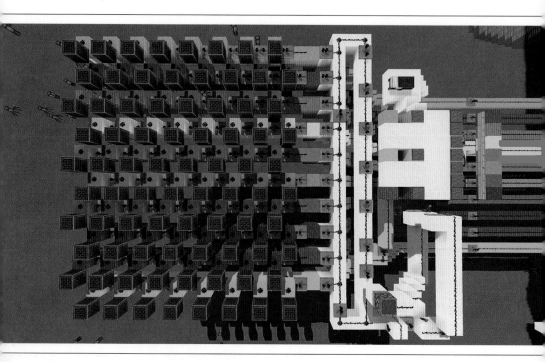

Motion Madness:
Redstone Mechs & Machines

There are two type of builders: those who use Redstone extensively, and those who look at it like some sort-of mystery magic force. Among those that can actually do complex things with Redstone, there are those that are pretty darn good at it, and then there are the guys in this section.

To call these guys masters of Redstone is maybe even a disservice: they are (sometimes literally) electrical engineers and inventive wizards. What they can make this game do with just a few simple tools and wires is nothing short of astounding, and so it's no surprise that their maps

have become some of the more widely distributed and endlessly played there are. The first time you get even a little bored of the game, or wonder what could possibly be done more than what you already have, these are the maps you want to check out.

Editor's note: Redstone is very tricky and particular, so sometimes when these maps don't install or render right, or if you load them in the wrong version of Minecraft, they may not work. They should with a little tweaking, so if you download, just make sure you read all the instructions and check online for help.

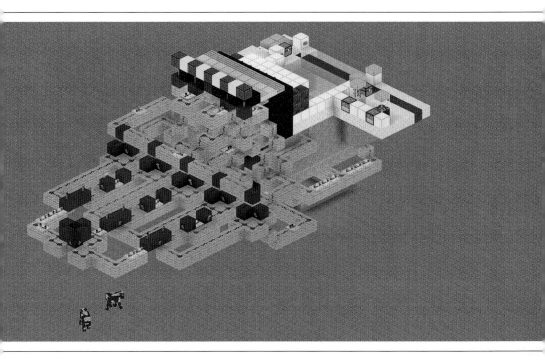

100% Working Bowling Alley

By ACtennisAC: Despite this Bowling Alley being born during the 1.5 update, the Redstone is so solid that it still seems to work totally fine in even the most recent update. It is fun, utilizing "balls" (ball-shaped items like Enderpearls etc.) that you throw across an ice floor, allowing them to slide into slots in front of the "pins" (a single Fence piece).

When you put the balls into the holes before the pins, said pin drops down and is scored, just like in real bowling! That's not all though, as this is a complete alley and also features a sort-of cotton candy machine and a popcorn machine which both actually dispense items to players.

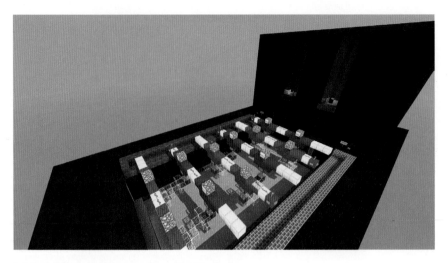

Working Foosball Table

By SethBling: SethBling is widely considered one of the top 5, if not the top, Redstone builder in the history of the game. This foosball table alone is enough to earn him consideration for the title, and though it is one of our favorites of his, it's certainly not his only piece of Redstone magic.

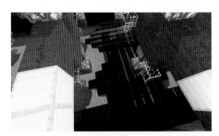

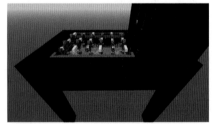

So how does it work? Welp, all you have to do is press the button to drop a ball onto the surface (pretty much the same concept as that of the Bowling Alley), and then players on either side of the table use buttons on their "men" which drop a short burst of Water down that moves the ball in the direction of the flow.

When the balls reach the goals, they score for your team, and (if installed right) your goal is marked automatically on the board! So, so much fun!

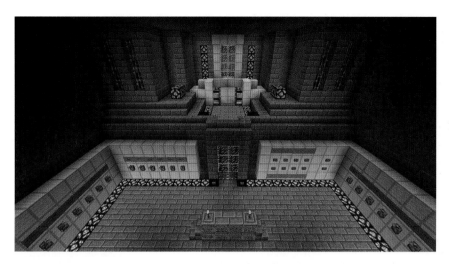

CNB's Batcave!

By CNBMinecraft: Many houses utilize Redstone here and there, whether for auto Doors, traps or Dispensers, but there aren't many that can do what CNBMinecraft's Batcave can do. This cave might not have an Alfred or a Batmobile, but what it does have is a Redstone clock, an automatic item stack dispenser and even a storage facility, which utilizes Minecarts that can be used to store stuff in and then be sent away and called back at will.

Here you see the dispenser, which allows you to choose an item type and various amounts of said item, which will be automatically dispensed.

It's a good sight better than your basic dispensing system, and we can imagine the necessary Redstone (which is hidden in this build) is extensive and complex.

Color the Sheep

By codecrafted: Another legendary Redstoner (who, if we had space, would certainly have gone in our Hall of Fame), codecrafted's mini-games tend to be highly inventive and stylized. Color the Sheep is no exception, for it is a game in which players take Dyes of a different color each and attempt to dye as much of the sheep as possible.

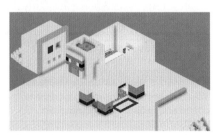

Whoever dyes the most, wins, and then you can reset the game. The Sheep itself is full of Redstone, as is the accessible underground area. If you'd like to see how a master does it, this is a good map to take a look at.

This Sheep does not know what's about to hit it. It's colors. Colors will hit this Sheep.

Disco Archery

By FVDisco: Along with SethBling, FVDisco is one of the most famous and prolific Redstone professionals in the world. Here we have disco (he also goes by his shortened name)'s very fun automatic archery range.

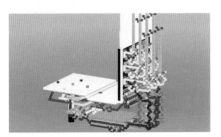

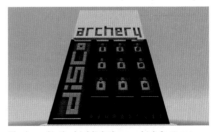

What's awesome about disco is that not only is he inventive, he's also one of the most efficient wire-rs out there. Just look at how little was needed here compared to some of the other builds we've highlighted!

The board is the highlight here, which features randomly popping-up targets which are auto-counted when hit *and* auto-reset when done.

Interactive Computer

By Igor_Timofeev: This build would be cool looking even if it didn't work, as it's a lazer-accurate representation of the computer model in question. However, get this: it actually types and displays your typing on its screen!

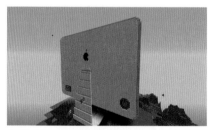

And look! It does all of that while maintaining its slim form up top.

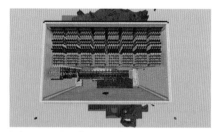

In fact, Igor_Timofeev says that he did this entire thing with wiring, not using any moving mechanisms at all, which is downright mind-boggling to even us who know a little about Redstone.

Mineception

By codecrafted: Another codecrafted product, the concept here is that you can actually play a Minecraft-like game *within Minecraft*. Thus the name: Mineception.

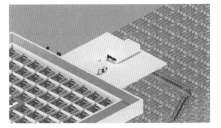

It's a bit of a tricky one to get to work, but when you do, it's very cool. You are able to build with 8 different blocks, and it even incorporates moving water and gravity.

This is one of those that we literally have no idea how it works or how to even begin to make something like this, and for that it has certainly earned its place among the best Redstone builds.

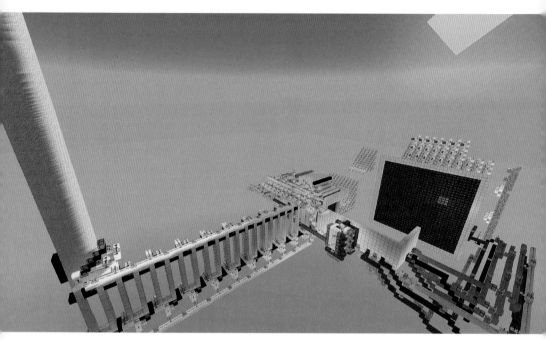

Paint 2.0

By FillzMinecraft: Speaking of wild Redstone that we just can't figure out the workings of, this Paint 2.0 map is somewhat similar to the Interactive Computer in that it allows you to create and display things on a screen.

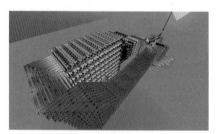

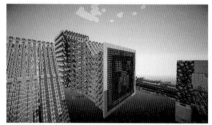

What's different, however, is that instead of typing, this program is used to draw items on the screen. It has a moving cursor that is controlled from buttons, and it works pretty darn quickly despite the huge number of parts it features.

Maybe even more amazing, it can actually save a few of your designs, allowing you to recall them without having to destroy your current work. Too darn cool, FillzMinecraft.

Piston Driven 12hr Digital Clock

By CNBMinecraft: You might recognize this from his Batcave, but we liked CNBMinecraft's clock so much that we felt it deserved its own spot in our gallery. Using what seems like really not enough Redstone (meaning- how in the heck did he do that??), this clock continuously displays the actual accurate game-time.

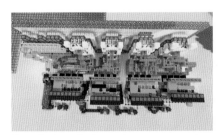

Forget having to look up at the moon ever again, this clock is accurate and thoroughly useful, allowing you to really get a quick answer to how much safe, safe daylight you have left. Of course, you might want to put this someplace where a Creeper can't get to it. Just sayin'.

What's even better about this here map is that CNBMinecraft was nice enough to build both a working version of his clock and the various pieces that are required to build it, showing you exactly how it's done. We love that idea, and we hope more builds take after this one!

Playable Guitar

By FVDisco: Another disco build, this guitar is actually capable of playing 10 different chords through using Pressure Plates and a whole dang lot of Redstone. In fact, disco went all out and created a whole darn band's worth of instruments in this way; just check out the Programmable Drum Kit on the next page!

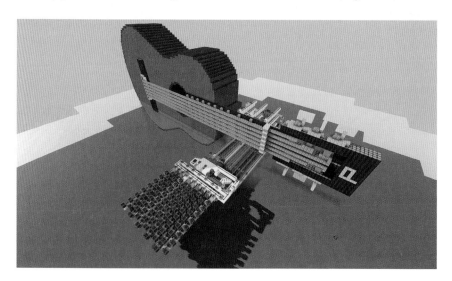

Programmable Drum Kit

By FVDisco: Not only does this build have an amazing look, with a bit of quirkiness and all necessary pieces for a real kit, it also plays actual music.

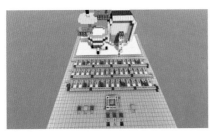

This is another one that just blows our mind trying to comprehend, even more-so because this kit can actually be programmed with three different channels.

FVDisco also has a piano among his other builds, and we'd love to see someone get together a little Minecraft band with all three on the same world. Would be pretty cool, no?

RDF ASCII Word Processor

By berick: We've included another word processor in addition to the Interactive Computer in order to showcase the fact that the same thing can be done in entirely different ways. Instead of going with the aesthetic look of the other build, this one is all about functionality.

As opposed to the Glowstone of the Interactive Computer, this processor uses Redstone Torches to display its typing.

Aaaaaand, this is the stuff that makes it work. That is some serious, serious Redstoning.

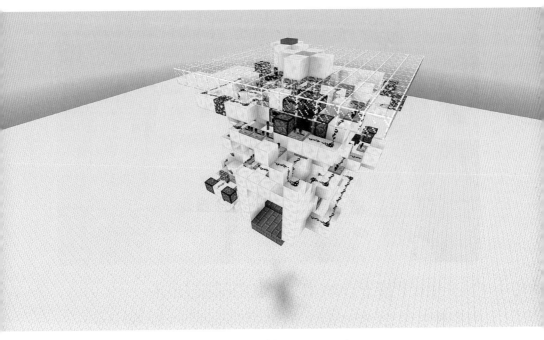

Secret Base (With 'Yolo' Exit!)

By MinecraftPG5: A fourth legend of the 'Stone, MinecraftPG5 is a group that tends to manage to do things that no one else can quite so well with the material. What we have here is actually a few different mechanisms, all tied up into one base.

The basic mechanism here is that this base has an entrance that is entirely hidden and is only activated by placing a Redstone torch in exactly the right block, which itself can be totally hidden from view. For those wanting to keep their base a secret, this is ideal.

The base itself is pretty expansive and has a very James Bond feel to it, but the awesome doesn't end there. In the back of the base is something that becomes the show stealer for this build: the YOLO exit, which uses controlled TNT detonations to absolutely launch you up and out of the base, closing a second secret portal behind you as you leave.

SUPER Pig Powered Slot Machine

By FVDisco Yes yes, we know, there's a lot of FVDisco on here, but that's just because his builds are not only awesome to play, they're also just too cool-looking not to show 'em off. For instance, these here pigslots!

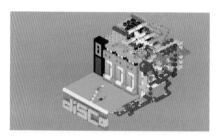

Disco could have just make a simple slot machine, but instead, they added an amazing cartoony carnival-game look to this working game that elevates it from cool to classic.

Here's how and what you win, according to disco:

1 Diamond gets you = 9 credits
3 Lapis blocks = 2 diamonds
3 Gold blocks = 6 diamonds
3 Diamond blocks = 30 diamonds

Tree-Eater Tree Farm

By Cubehamster: So far most of our builds have been just cool or amazing, but this one is actually incredibly practical and useful, utilizing Redstone in a cube-ish area that could be fairly easily incorporated into your own builds.

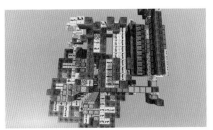

But what does all this do? It chops trees and creates Wood for ya! No longer do you have to go out hunting, this baby does it all for you and will continuously provide you with the materials you need.

Many versions of this kind of thing exist out there (though for Wood cutting this is probably our fave), so if there's a process you'd like to make easier in the 'Craft, do some Googling; there's probably a machine out there for just what you want.

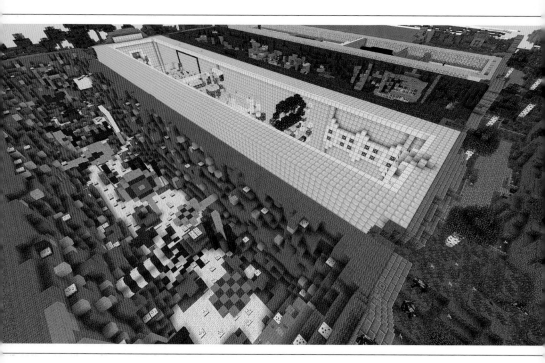

Awesome Arenas:
Melee Maps, Skyblock & More

Whether Notch and the Mojang crew ever meant it to originally, one of the most popular parts of the game of Minecraft these days are the competitive maps and challenge maps that have arisen. These maps use the features, quirks and rules of the game and turn it from being a game about co-op survival into something else entirely with all new goals.

What those goals are and how you get to them depend on the mini-game and/ or map, and there are nearly endless of these. From straight up Player vs. Player (PvP) maps to co-operative building areas with restrictions and goals like Skyblock, people have gotten unbelievably creative with Minecraft, especially in recent years. There's even a zombie apocalypse mini-game and one where you play as a prisoner! Here are some maps you can download and use with your friends to introduce an entirely new element or five to your games and servers.

Abyss

By CherryGoose_Studios: We kick off our list here with a classic-style challenge survival map by CherryGoose_Studios. This type of map is basic survival, except it typically has far fewer resources than normal in a much smaller space than you're used to.

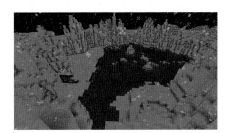

Not only are you trying to survive here, but you have a few tasks you can attempt to complete. In this case, your list includes such things as creating the two types of giant mushrooms, fixing the "north pole" and even getting to and killing the Ender Dragon. Those who complete the list have the knowledge that they are truly skilled at the game, and it's a pretty darn good feeling to beat one of these kind of maps.

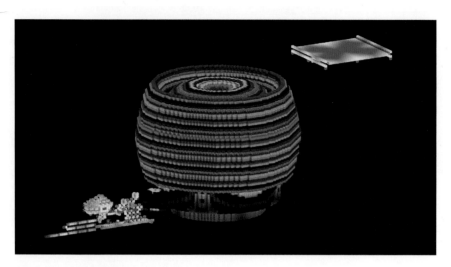

Bow Spleef Arena

By La_Pixel: SPLEEF! One of the iconic minigames of the 'Craft, Spleef is played like this: you and your competitors enter an arena whose floor is something easily broken such as Wool. Using whatever weapons or items you decide on (try it with Flint & Steel and Ender Pearls!), you all attack each other by knocking out the blocks beneath peoples' feet so they fall into the pit below.

This particular arena is has a playful and colorful design that gives the whole combat scene a great setting. There are oh so many variations on Spleef arenas out there, so if you get into this game, definitely do a spot of Googlin' to find some other great options.

Cluster Chunk PvP

By three_two: Cluster Chunk, like Spleef, is another PvP game, but the rules are very different. Instead of simply trying to kill players, you are trying to defend your own team's base while attacking that of the enemy. Whoever's team destroys the other team's Bed at the base first wins!

Of course doing that is no easy task, and Cluster Chunk is chock full of various mechanisms and locations that can be used to your advantage or against you.

You'll have to do a lot of building, a lot of combat and a lot of dying to win this game, and matches can get insanely heated and rather lengthy if players are pretty skilled. It's a great one to play with other people who are about at your level, and it's all-around one of the most solid PvP maps you can find.

Cops And Robbers

By Podcrash: Very similar to the popular Prison style of mini-game (in fact some Prison games are exactly like this one), Cops and Robbers is a style of play where one or more players are in charge (cops) and control the lives of the other players (robbers) who are in a prison-style building.

As the prisoners do what the cops say and go about their days, they must attempt to escape without attracting notice. Those that are noticed will be punished, and the game ends when either people escape or the cops have the players on total lockdown.

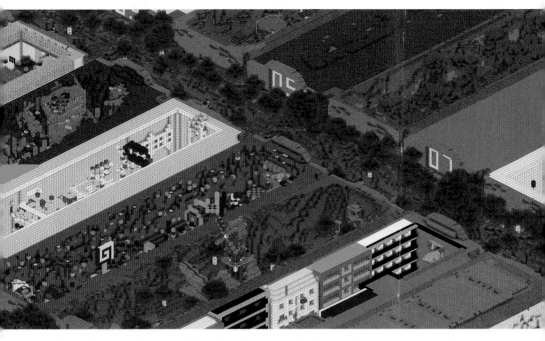

Parkour Map Christmas Calendar

By MinecraftPG5: Certainly one of the most popular types of mini-games, the concept of parkour is simple and easy to pick up, but hard to master. Essentially, it's just jumping and otherwise maneuvering from a starting point to a goal without falling. If you fall, you start over!

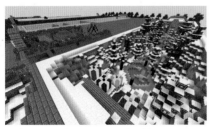

Parkour maps are set up to make this very difficult, and you will have to be incredibly accurate even to get very far at all into your map.

This particular map features a whole heap of various parkour areas, each with its own theme and difficulty level. It was created by the MinecraftPG5 group as a Christmas release, and it is an absolutely top-notch example of the parkour style.

SethBling's Minecraft TNT Olympics

By SethBling: Of course SethBling has created an awesome, totally unique style of mini-game! This one has an amazing setting, featuring a full-size Olympic arena with all sorts of mini-games.

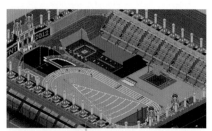

To be more specific, in SethBling's Minecraft TNT Olympics you can do: Javelin Throw, Trap Shooting, High Jump & Long Jump, 400m Hurdles and Gymnastics Vault, Crew (rowing), Balance beam, Synchronized Swimming and even Horse Riding!

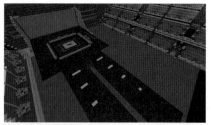

Here we see the Javelin Throw, one of the many awesome games this features. Though this isn't one you'll find on a lot of servers (probably due to its size), it's worth a look even just to see the amazing arena SethBling built.

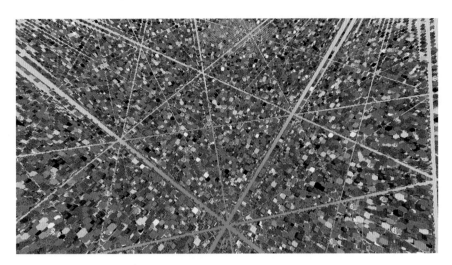

SkyGrid Surival Map

By guess who? SethBling again!: Yep, we're doubling down on the Bling, and that's because this mini-game is found on a huge number of servers, partially due to its unique look and partially because it's just really darn fun!

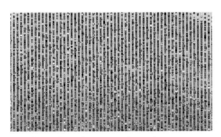

This shot is from the exact right angle so you can see how this grid is kind-of set up. The point of all of these individual gridded blocks is that there's just about every kind of block there is, plus a few secrets like hidden chests.

The rules? Whatever you want! You can do PvP, you can play survival, you can literally do whatever you want with the map. That's the awesomeness of it: it's just so well designed that it can be used in nearly infinite fun ways.

Skylands Parkour

By theKyleman: Parkour, but in the sky! No more cheating and no mercy for those who fall, Skylands Parkour is an ultimate parkour map.

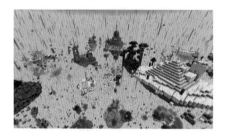

This parkour map is pretty open as to how you play, featuring a very extensive course that could be either just straight up parkour or a hybrid of skyblock/ survival and parkour.

Skyblock Warriors

By SwipeShotTeam: If we had to say what is the *most* popular mini-game style in the history of Minecraft, we'd be hard pressed to choose something other than Skyblock. The concept for this one is that you and other teams start on a very, very small piece of land with very few resources and you must use them to complete objectives before the other team and/or kill the other players.

You'll end up having to use such inventions as Cobblestone generators and more to make any headway, so this is definitely one that will hone your skills at the game. For that, and for the hours of fun it provides, we love skyblock.

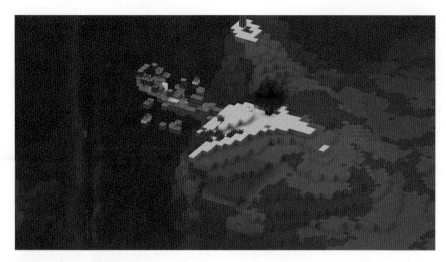

Survival Island

By YoursCrafter: Another iconic classic style of play, the idea here is that you are stranded on an island and must try and survive and thrive with what little you have.

In this particular iteration of the classic, you are shipwrecked on one island that is close to another that has a small shelter on it.

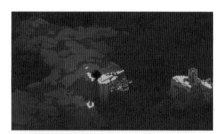

You only have the resources available on these two islands to do things with, which makes it surprisingly difficult to do much at all. You can play this a few ways, either just as classic survival or with some goals in mind, similar to skyblock.

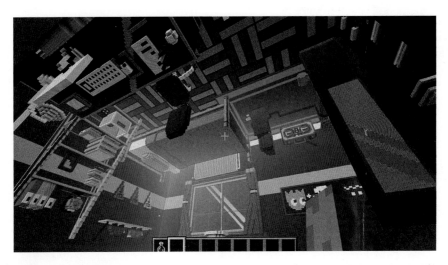

The Dropper

By Bigre: We might sound a bit like a skipping record player at this point, but this is another of the more well-known and extensively downloaded challenge maps. The concept is simple: you drop out of a hole and must fall through the area beneath it and get to the other side.

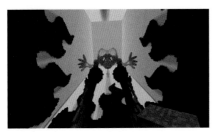

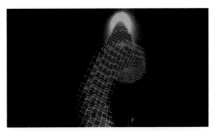

Each area is harder and harder, and they all have their own unique look and dangers. Here we've got a skeleton Dropper area. Watch out for those ribs!

The beginning of The Dropper (seen here) is so easy that anyone could get through it, but beware: it gets harder very quickly.

The Underground

By MinecraftPG5: Another challenge/survival map, The Underground is incredibly well designed, with a dark, underground, Gothic look to it that gives it a much more menacing feel than many others.

Among the very, very many challenges the creators have set for you are: collecting 512 Sand, Clay, Snowblocks and Iceblocks, finding various Spawners and building things like labyrinths and towers.

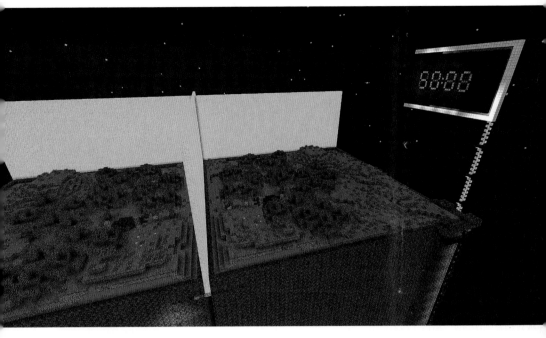

The Walls

By Hypixel: The beloved Hypixel came up with this concept, which is a variation of what is know as survival games, a concept based on *The Hunger Games* films where players are dropped into an arena with a natural environment.

In The Walls, players start in their own quadrant, and once the game starts, the walls are dropped and the players must start crafting, attacking and defending themselves. Last player alive wins! Oh yeah.

World In A Jar

By GTawesomesauce: Think skyblock challenge survival, but in jars! This map features a large number of carefully crafted jars, each of which contains a variety of different blocks and item types.

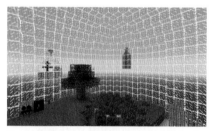

You start out in just one jar, and as you build and craft, you are eventually able to make your way to a second jar, and then a third.

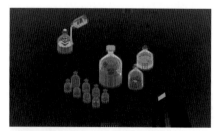

As with all of these kind of maps, there is a set list of goals, though of course you only have to follow them if you wish.

Zombie Siege

By FVDisco: We've had a SethBling, we've had a Hypixel, so of course we'll need a disco map in here as well. Disco makes some very neat mini-game maps that, unsurprisingly, make extensive use of Redstone to make them automated.

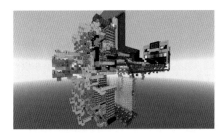

Extensive use of Redstone we said.

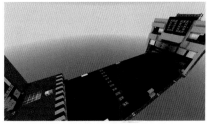

This map's mini-game pits players against waves of Zombies that keep coming, and you are armed with TNT cannons and your own wits. Survive and feel awesome! But, you probably won't. Zombies bite hard y'all.

Pixel Pushers:
Painting With Blocks

Besides Redstone geniuses, there's another type of builder out there that does something pretty amazing that not all Crafters can A- even do (mostly due to the amount of patience it takes), and and B- are actually any good at.

That is the style that is called pixel art, which is exactly what it sounds like: players use blocks of various colors to create images one block at a time. Yep, it takes forever, even with the aid of computer programs to tell you exactly where to put each block (not everyone uses these, though). If Minecraft is a medium, this is kind-of like a medium within a medium, and people have made some very cool stuff with it over the years. While saying what is "the best" pixel art is as subjective as saying what the "best" painting is, these are some examples of the various styles that are out there to give you an idea of what is being done with this kind of play.

FireDragon

By MultiShorty00: A nice fire dragon done up pixel-wise, this is a very good use of the different colored Wool blocks from the game.

Some pixel art looks weird at angles, but this one still looks pretty darn good.

Mona Lisa

By CrystalBlocks: Has to be seen in-game to really get the effect, this Mona Lisa copy is MASSIVE at 116,760 blocks.

When you get up close you can see that not only are Wool blocks used, but also regular blocks from the games like Pumpkins, which add some shading to the pixel.

Radiance Of Circles

By Palaeos: Palaeos builds their art in a bit of a different style, preferring abstract shapes and symmetry to representations of figures or items.

These kind of works often end up incorporated into bigger builds as decoration, such as a floor or a floating design.

Playing around with two-dimensional builds like this can really enhance your aesthetic work on other, more structural-style builds.

Hessen Banner

By Elwyryn: The traditional Hessen or Hessian coat of arms recreated by Elwyryn.

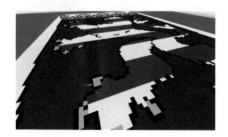

If you can think of drawing it in the real world, it can probably be at least approximated in Minecraft. As always, the only limit is your imagination (and the amount of free time you have).

Dragon

By game3player: Another style of dragon, this shows how drawing with pixels can be done in just as many styles as drawing by hand.

This one was almost too big to render all at once! The cool thing about pixel art is you can resize most pieces to whatever you need, whether large or small.

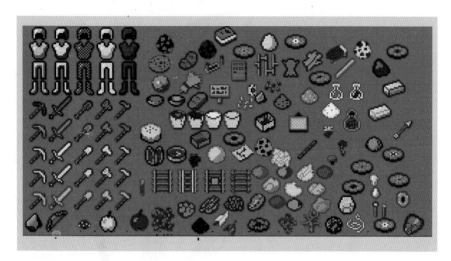

Item Wall

By XylClan: Since everything in Minecraft is already made out of blocks, which are basically 3D pixels, and the textures on those blocks are themselves made out of pixels, it's pretty easy to recreate icons and even items from Minecraft with its own blocks (though obviously they will be much much larger than the real thing).

XylClan added the extra feature of making these bits of pixel art 3D, which makes this giant item wall pop both literally and figuratively.

Slender Man

by bh991: If you don't know what the Slender Man is, we invite you to do a bit of Internet research and get yourself good and scared of this (probably) mythical creature. This Slender Man build by bh991 is something we really like, primarily because it uses the pixel's naturally blocky shape as part of the aesthetic instead of trying to use enough pixels to make the piece look like it actually has curves.

It reminds us of characters from old games like the Monkey Island series, when characters looked like this because they had to. Creators back then tapped into something cool when they became masters of character creation with just a few pixels, and we think bh991 has found that same rich vein of aesthetics with this build.

block☆rocking
blockrocking.tumblr.com

Hall Of Fame:
Master Builder Spotlights

As it is with all mediums, anyone can pick up Minecraft, but to perfect it takes countless hours of dedication and not just a little bit of skill. It's a big, complex game, and while learning every little thing about it is probably impossible, there are some builders out there who have honed their craft with the 'Craft to a point where their creations leave people in awe all over the planet.

The debate on who the "best" builder is rages pretty fiercely in certain parts of the Minecraft world, but with so very many ways to be good at the game, and so very many different styles out there, we think there's really no way to ever answer that question. However, what we certainly can do is find some truly skilled and inspiring builders to respect and honor for their accomplishments.

Blockrocking

Link: blockrocking.tumblr.com/

Focus: Tall, monument-esque builds with modern architecture and a sci-fi influence. Often incorporates nature juxtaposed against the modern feel.

Downloadable?: No

Though each of Blockrocking's builds look significantly different from each other, these tall structures that incorporate a lot of plain Stone (in a way that makes it seem fresh again), glass and greenery placed high above the ground make this skilled and not-too-well-known builder's style immediately recognizable.

Blockrocking

"I build on smp servers and render the results and work in progress in Chunky and post it on my site."

Carloooo

"Yes. Finally! I have constructed a spawn worthy of the gods!"

Link:
planetminecraft.com/member/carloooo/

Focus: Madcap and wildly inventive builds of all kinds, often with a military focus.

Downloadable?: Yes

Carloooo is a bit of a double-edged sword as a builder: not only are they consistently putting out builds that resemble no-one else's and which feature a thrilling level of detail, they're also one of the funniest Minecrafters online. Seriously, head on over to carloooo's page on PlanetMinecraft and just try not to laugh at the hilarious descriptions of the creations. We'd say you should then give one a download and try it out, but we doubt we'll really have to once you get there and see how awesome this talented builder's worlds are.

Circleight

"Each and every one of us have something different going on in our lives, so just keep in mind it's all about what you enjoy, not others. In your own unique little world, you're the best at what you do and you're the only one doing it."

Link:
planetminecraft.com/member/circleight/

Focus: Enormous, colorful builds full of sweeping architecture and surprising stylistic choices. Truly original.

Downloadable?: Yes

There's really no one like Circleight in the building game. When you talk about inventiveness, detail, color and size of builds, that conversation simply cannot be had without talking about this lady. She is an artist, no question about it, and her builds are testaments to what the power of the human imagination can do when given a few tools to work with. Circleight, you are a pusher of boundaries and an inspiration to the community.

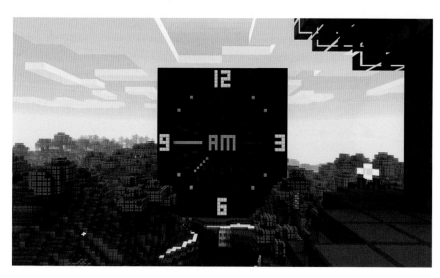

FVDisco

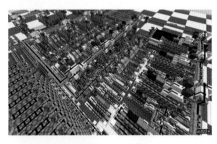

"Interesting fact: The original Temple of Notch required you to sacrifice a pig to gain audience with him......a little creepy."

Links: ocddisco.com

youtube.com/user/FVDisco

Focus: Brilliant Redstone creator, highly stylized, and also built one of the best custom texture packs available.

Downloadable?: Yes

Oh FVDisco, we owe you and your Redstone majesty so much for the many hours of gleeful fun you've given us in this game of building. As one of the world's premier Redstone mechanics and certainly one of the most well-known and universally loved builders, FVDisco is a hero of the game and a pioneer of the realm of Minecraft possibilities.

Hydraxus

Links:
planetminecraft.com/member/hydraxus

youtube.com/user/TheHydraxus

Focus: Temples and castles with sweeping, complex architecture.

Downloadable?: Yes

Some people just get fantasy and fantastical architecture right. Hydraxus is not only one of those people, they're one of the people that those who also get it right look to for inspiration in their own builds. Minecraft's community is rife with folks attempting decent fantasy builds, but Hydraxus shows us what can happen when you really master the style.

"If you set your brightness to moody, take a night vision potion and set it to night time, you get a really purple cool effect."

Hypixel (and Team)

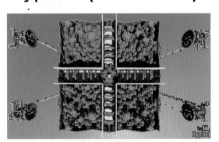

"Having a server like mine is so much fun, the only downside is that sleep is a thing of the past!"

Links: hypixel.net

youtube.com/user/Hypixel

Focus: Some of the best arenas, adventure and combat maps available, plus runs a server of impeccable quality.

Downloadable?: Oh yes (one of the most popular)

Special Tools: MCEdit, NBTEdit

If you can think of a challenge-style type of map, Hypixel has probably built a near-perfect version of it, and in fact he might even be the inventor of it. Creator of The Walls and many, many other classic maps, Hypixel is one of Minecraft's biggest and boldest personalities. Often found on his own server, where they frequently throw events, Hypixel is a major force in the Minecraft community due to his immense skill-set when it comes to builds of all types, but most especially those that allow players to have a bit of competition with each other.

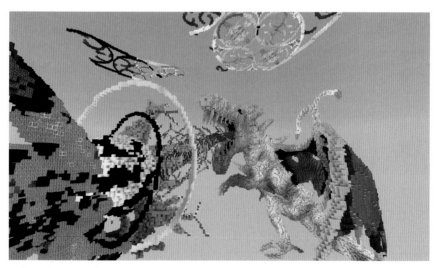

Murps

"I know a lot of people who make organics try to be precise with their curves, but I am not like that. It is hard to describe what I do, but I just place blocks quickly and somewhat randomly, while knowing how to make precise curves and lines in the project. It takes a lot of practice to understand how to make curves quickly and natural. "

Link:
planetminecraft.com/member/murps/

Focus: Fantastical and thoroughly imaginative mega-builds.

Downloadable?: Yes

Special Tools: Voxelsniper

If Hydraxus is amazing at fantasy architecture, Murps takes the cake when it comes to building fantasy maps with a spirit of adventure and freedom to them. Utilizing nature, color and organic-looking styles into their excellent fantastical builds, Murps creates environments that could not have come from any other builder. For perhaps the best example of what can happen when you let your creativity run wild on a build, check out Murps' Eternal Haven, or if you want a lesson in crafting organically, their character builds on PlanetMinecraft feature some very helpful instructional guides and notes on Murps' style, showing you how the magic is made step-by-step.

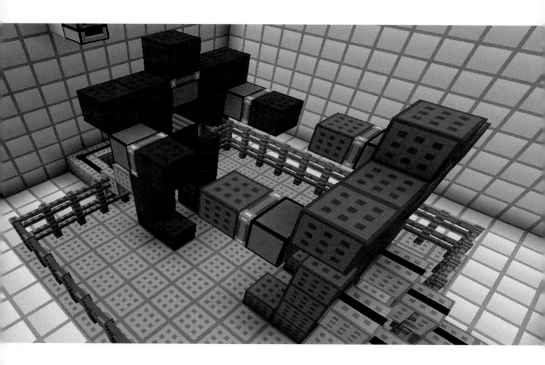

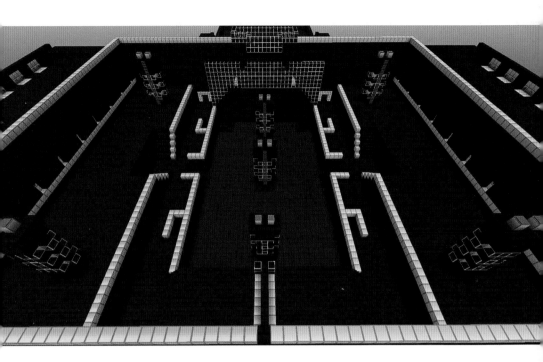

SethBling

Links: sethbling.com

youtube.com/user/sethbling

Focus: Insane Redstone genius, also makes Minecraft mods and tools for builds.

Downloadable?: Oh yes
(also crazy popular

"I make Minecraft inventions, tutorials and creations. Especially videogame and board game recreations."

Not that many players can say that not only are they pretty good at Minecraft, but that they've also created maps that became an entire genre of mini-game. SethBling, however, can do just that. As one of the best Redstoners around, plus just a super-talented all-around builder and one of the game's real celebrities, SethBling has carved out a name for himself in Minecraft by putting out one solid, thoroughly addictive map after another, and you'll find his work (maybe without knowing it) on servers everywhere.

TheHexBox

"Sometimes simple is better."

Link: youtube.com/user/TheHexBox

Focus: Highly modern homes with a touch of nature, often set in a lovely sunny landscape.

Downloadable?: Yes

Special Tools: Chunky (for rendering)

Specializing in a certain part of Minecraft is something that most people do to one degree or another, but TheHexBox's dedication to becoming a better and better modern home-builder is not only admirable, it's also led to the player becoming one of Minecraft's golden children of the modern house build. All of TheHexBox's homes are fully built with care and precision, both inside and out, and they've had Minecrafters world-wide going back to the drawing board to spruce up their own creations for years now.

TheHexBox

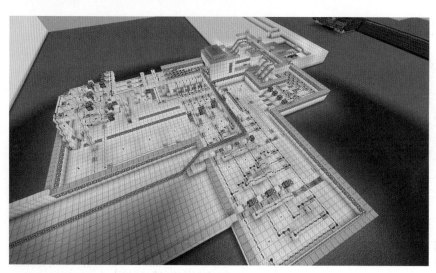

MinecraftPG5

"(We are) electrical engineering students and professional redstoners in Minecraft."

Links:
planetminecraft.com/member/
minecraftpg5/

youtube.com/user/minecraftpg5

Focus: Redstone magician group, working with everything from mini-games to adventure maps to gadgets.

Downloadable?: Yes

Since Redstone is pretty much just a simplified version of real electric wiring (but less likely to zap you painfully), it should come as no surprise that a group of electrical engineers would put out some of the most efficient, awesome and dare we say elegant Redstone builds in history. We love these guys for their passion and dedication to not just making Redstone work, but making it work as well as it possibly could. For those looking for lessons in wiring, these are your guys.